Olya Yarosh

RELENTLESS

Real stories of real women
and their extraordinary faith

Bright Books, 2019

Relentless: True Stories of Ordinary Women of Extraordinary Faith by Olya Yarosh ©2019 Olya Yarosh. Translated and revised from the Russian language version published in Europe. All rights reserved.

ISBN 978-617-7766-07-9

All Scripture quotations, unless otherwise indicated, are taken from the Holy Bible, New International Version®, NIV®. Copyright ©1973, 1978, 1984, 2011 by Biblica, Inc.™ Used by permission of Zondervan. All rights reserved worldwide. www.zondervan.com The "NIV" and "New International Version" are trademarks registered in the United States Patent and Trademark Office by Biblica, Inc.™

Scripture quotations marked HCSB are taken from the Holman Christian Standard Bible®, Copyright © 1999, 2000, 2002, 2003, 2009 by Holman Bible Publishers. Used by permission. Holman Christian Standard Bible®, Holman CSB®, and HCSB® are federally registered trademarks of Holman Bible Publishers.

Scripture quotations marked (KJV) are taken from the KING JAMES VERSION, public domain.

Scripture quotations marked (NKJV) are taken from the NEW KING JAMES VERSION®. Copyright© 1982 by Thomas Nelson, Inc. Used by permission. All rights reserved.

Scripture quotations marked (AMP) are taken from the Amplified Bible, Copyright © 1954, 1958, 1962, 1964, 1965, 1987 by The Lockman Foundation. Used by permission.

Scripture quotations marked (NLT) are taken from THE HOLY BIBLE, NEW LIVING TRANSLATION, Copyright© 1996, 2004, 2007 by Tyndale House Foundation. Used by permission of Tyndale House Publishers, Inc., Carol Stream, Illinois 60188. All rights reserved. Used by permission.

Scripture quotations marked (OANT) are taken from The Original Aramaic New Testament in Plain English by David Bauer.

Scripture quotations marked (NASB) are taken from the NEW AMERICAN STANDARD BIBLE®, Copyright © 1960,1962,1963,1968,1971,1972,1973,1975,1977,1995 by The Lockman Foundation. Used by permission.

Scripture quotations marked (NCV) are taken from the New Century Version®. Copyright © 2005 by Thomas Nelson. Used by permission. All rights reserved.

Illustrations by Vera Mishchuk

TABLE OF CONTENTS

Thank You 4
Introduction 6
Forward 9
  1. Mom. The Faith of Hope 15
  2. Jochebed. Victory of the Slaves 31
  3. Hannah. Tit for Tat 51
  4. Julia. A Song of a Daughter 71
  5. Eve. Life After Death 91
  6. Hagar. Anguish Misdirected 111
  7. Sveta. The Brightness of Her Soul 131
  8. Esther. Beauty Within 149
  9. Martha. Fear vs. Faith 169
10. Oksana. New Marriage—Same Husband 191
11. Five Daughters of Zelophehad.
    A Case for Social Justice 207
12. Naomi. The Joy of Second Chances 225
13. Grandmother. Faithfulness to the Ends of the Earth . . . 245
14. A Slow-Paced Race 265
Marathon 273

THANK YOU

I would have never been able to write this book if it were not for my personal encounter with the Lord and if I were not surrounded by my own great cloud of witnesses.

Therefore, I am forever indebted to my heavenly Father, my Savior Jesus Christ, and the Holy Spirit.

I am thankful to my loving husband, Vasily Yarosh, for his never-ceasing devotion, encouragement, and faith in me. You're my best friend!

I am grateful to my darlings, my precious children, my daughters and my son—Katerina Anna, Paul William, and Ariana Joy. You are my inspiration, my strength, and my joy. I love you with all my heart!

I am grateful beyond words and adoration to my beloved parents, who surrounded me with forty-two years of love, acceptance, and steadfast prayers. Pavel and Nadezhda Okara, you lift me up and inspire me!

My lifelong best friends, my dearest sisters—Verusya, Annechka, Irochka, and Anastasia. My loving, honest, sincere, inspiring, and always-thinking-of-others sisters! I love you!

To all my family and friends! You've touched my heart so deeply. You are my biggest blessings and my lessons, teaching me through tears and joy. Only eternity will reveal to us how much, when, and where we have made this impact on each other; we have blessed, unearthed, polished, revealed, sharpened, healed, comforted, nudged, and inspired one another. Because of you, my life is made beautiful!

Dearest women whose stories I have already written or dream about writing! Your lives are so inspiring, and I believe they will inspire those who will read your stories. You are my great cloud of witnesses!

And a special thank you to my friend Vera Mishchuk for translating this book into English. You didn't just translate the words; you've heard my heart and carried its message, passing it right through your own heart. I shall cherish this greatly!

Finally, I am grateful to my editor, Libby Gontarz, for your attention to the smallest detail, I am touched by the fact that you not only fixed the misspellings and punctuation but you cared deeply about this book.

In conclusion, I am beyond thankful to my publisher "Bright Books" for their patient and thorough guidance and for their wholehearted approach to getting this work published.

INTRODUCTION

> Therefore, since we are surrounded by such a great cloud of witnesses, let us throw off everything that hinders and the sin that so easily entangles. And let us run with perseverance the race marked out for us, fixing our eyes on Jesus, the pioneer and perfecter of faith. For the joy set before him he endured the cross, scorning its shame, and sat down at the right hand of the throne of God. Consider him who endured such opposition from sinners, so that you will not grow weary and lose heart. (Hebrews 12:1–3)

Life is a journey. The two most important dates in our life are spread apart by a short dash, making that punctuation mark the shortest but most accurate representation of life. Each of us has our own journey—our own unique route and a given length of time—but everyone, without exception, experiences life like an obstacle course with trials and challenges to overcome. Yet it looks as if everyone thinks that we are the only ones running it, that we are all alone, as if we are the pioneers, and no one has ever gone through this before. A feeling that no one cares about us is the biggest lie of the enemy of our souls, and I think he has successfully forced this lie on humanity. But none of it is true! The Word of God is full of assurances that our heavenly Father loves us without limit, Jesus proved His love, and He abides in us and with us by his Holy Spirit. And his Spirit reminds us to lift our heads and look up, look around—for you are surrounded by a great cloud of witnesses!

As I write these lines and as you read them, this proves that we are still en route. We have already gone a good distance, and only God knows what awaits us in the near future.

Ever since childhood, I have been and continue to be inspired by many well-known Bible stories, stories of different women, each with her own unique fate and struggles. Troubles and trials, suffering and illness, even the death of loved ones—all these would attempt to break their spirit and destroy their faith, love, and hope. But none of them would relent. They speak from the pages of my Bible just as clearly and shine just as brightly as my contemporary heroines: my grandmother, my mom, my friends and those wonderful women whom I have yet to meet in the next few decades, God willing. All of them have this one thing in common: They were personally and intimately acquainted with the One Who conquered hell and death, and through his victory, they were able to attain victory in their own lives. These ones who went before us are a great cloud of witnesses. The Lord tells us, "Look at the great cloud of witnesses, and patiently continue on your journey." Jesus reigns victorious, and he lives within us; therefore, it is our destiny to finish this obstacle course, our life's journey, not to yield in determination or weaken in vigor but to remain *RELENTLESS*.

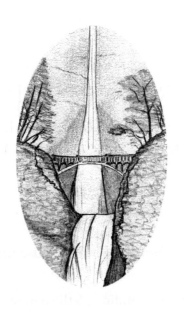

FORWARD
A GREAT CLOUD OF WITNESSES: THOSE WHO WENT BEFORE US

Saturday. Family. Sunrise. Rise and shine.

All five of us are standing on the parking lot at the bottom of the trail leading up to the mountains. A hike to the top of the beautiful waterfall with a very fitting and equally beautiful name, Angel's Rest. The views from up top will be breathtaking for sure. We stop to read the information stand: The height of the falls is 1,450 feet, which is equal to the height of a skyscraper 134 stories tall. The length of the round trip trail is only 4.8 miles. *What? Only ten thousand steps? That should be—easy!*

We line up into our "marching sandwich," a habit we created when our kids were still very little. Each child picks a spot, to be the ham, the cheese, the tomato, or the lettuce. The parents are always the bread. Dad walks in the front, the kids in the middle with Mom at the end, making sure no one gets lost.

We start off full of enthusiasm as the beautiful hiking path winds through towering evergreen fir trees. After about half an hour, the steep slope opens on the left side of the trail, where nothing grows because it is littered by massive sharp, gray rocks. I cringe from feeling uneasy as I look up at the rock face on the right, imagining the rockslide that has happened here. The kids are overjoyed to see our tiny car parked way down below. How did we get up here so fast? A few minutes later we are listening to the sound of the waterfall, then we cross the stream, and as we step off the little bridge, we jump back with a wild yelp. A black snake about a yard long with a bright yellow line going down its back has just slithered across right in front of us! *Brrr*.

Then come the questions.

"Mom, it's getting hot; are you sure that we have to go all the way up to the very top?"

"Did we take enough water with us?"

"Are you sure you want to go there and back?"

"Will we make it?"

We stop midway to catch our breath and to admire the tops of the giant fir trees, Highway 84 directly beneath us.

The towering evergreen trunks are right within our reach, and I run my hand against the roughness of the bark. Someone has carved a heart on one tree with their initials in the middle—A&V—and 1992 under the letters. I wonder if this was a site of a romantic proposal and if the girl had said her tearful but jubilant yes to the happy young man, and then as she was still wiping her tears, he had carved this perfect heart shape in the trunk of the massive evergreen tree. I wonder if they have got married somewhere not too far from where we live and, if they did, how old their children would be about now.

A couple with dogs walk by us as we take in the views below, then a family with two babies followed by a lone older man and a thin young man with his girlfriend who look like students or tourists from Asia. They were loudly chirping in Chinese and taking lots of pictures.

"You know, I saw a picture of Anya standing up there," I tell my kids. "She was standing here with her son and daughter, right on top of that rock." I point to the very top of the trail. I am out of breath and I blame it on my age. Anya is ten years younger, but our children are the same age. So I should make no excuses—we are definitely going all the way up!

Everyone is going up, with only a few coming down the path. They made it to the very top. Anya was there too. So we can do it.

And we do! There at the top, we sit on the edge of those massive jugged rocks, looking down at the majestic Columbia River that separates Oregon State from Washington. We look at the mountain range on the opposite side of the river and at Beacon

Rock—a tall lonesome giant, a volcanic rock formation that we have already climbed a few months before. All this beauty lies before us from the height of a 134-story building. I wanted to be still, soaking in this beauty. Then, I stand with my arms spread wide letting the warm air rush through my fingers. These two hours in the heat, climbing upward, walking by four snakes and on the rugged edges of the cliff are worth my every step because of this reward.

Fatigue. Obscurity. Danger. Fear. Someone has been there before us, and we can rest assured that we also can overcome every obstacles in our way. Those who have gone before us can teach us how.

Himalayas. Everest. You can read stories about unimaginable difficulties the climbers of these peaks have overcome: the lack of oxygen, bitter cold, storms, and avalanches. These are horror stories about frozen bodies along mountain paths. Some made it to the top, while others didn't. More turned back in time, but the unlucky few continued on their way, never to return.

We can learn even from those who have failed. They can teach us what not to do. One in a million will decide to conquer Mount Everest, so we put those stories on the shelf; after all, we won't really be needing them. But for those living in the beautiful Pacific Northwest, we all can have a chance to master a short hike to a mountaintop just outside our city on this coming Saturday. You can do it on any given week of the fifty-two in the year; every week that has a Monday inevitably ends on a Saturday—it being our small reward for all the hard work. When it comes to us humans, this type of heroism is available to us daily. And if Anya and Olya could do it, so can you.

Of course, this book is not about mountain climbing, although it is, but of a different kind. It is about life itself. Life is a climb: we start at birth and end when we die. Absolutely everyone will be on this journey. And although our starting point has nothing to do with us as we are born into different environments, it is within our will to make choices of where and how we go on this journey. It is within our power to stop and compare maps.

And yes, many will stumble, even fall. Some may become lost, losing sight of meaningful landmarks and spending years walking in circles. Others know for sure where they are going, and they will reach their goals. But absolutely everyone needs company, someone to share the journey with, to find encouragement and inspiration and an example to follow. And it is precisely these examples and this kind of support that we find in those around us as well as on the pages of our Bible. We read, *Don't despair, have courage, you will make it! Yes you can!*

Keep your eyes on Jesus! And look at the people who have gone before you; more often than not, their eyes were turned in the same direction. We can see Jesus in the lives of the people who have gone this way before, and seeing their journey, we are being greatly encouraged.

Look at this great cloud of witnesses all around you!

MOM.
THE FAITH OF HOPE

Grandma and Grandpa gave my mother a name that is perfect for her: Nadezhda—Hope. But in all honesty, we think a three-part name, Faith-Hope-Love, would have fit her even better. Needless to say, that is exactly what we mean when we call her Mom.

Mom is thirty-one years old and pregnant with her fifth child. She already has two sons and two daughters; who could this next child be? It doesn't seem too distant, but back then the baby's sex was revealed at birth, and the family couldn't see the baby for almost a week, until mother and baby were discharged from the hospital. Mom packed her hospital bag with swaddling blankets, a white duvet (comforter), a white lace "corner" to cover a blanket, and two rolls of ribbons: red for a girl and blue for a boy.

Anechka was born on September 28, 1986. She was a healthy, beautiful baby girl with big blue eyes.

The last months of Mom's pregnancy had been difficult, though, not only because of the swelling in her legs and the blistering summer's heat and not because of all the daily worries of taking care of our large family. In all honesty, cooking, cleaning, and doing laundry were the very last things on her mind. Her pregnancy was so difficult because night and day, my mother carried her baby daughter under her heart, all the while carrying her dying young son, Anton, in her arms above her belly.

On August 3, Anton, whom we lovingly called by his family pet name Antoshka, turned four. It was his last birthday.

When he was just six months old, my parents had noticed a strange, yellow-phosphorus glow in his eyes. After a doctor visit and urgent referral to an optometry specialist, my parents received a horrifying diagnosis: retinoblastoma, cancer of both eyes. The only option given was an operation, complete eye removal, in Moscow. But doctors warned that the tiny body of a nine-month-old baby could not survive the operation. On the other hand, if they waited for him to grow stronger, it would be too late to operate.

There was nothing the doctors could do. Or so they thought. Yet, we prayed and asked God to heal our Antoshka.

I remember those constant prayers in our house: long, loud, and sincere. Sometimes I, along with everyone, was kneeling in the hall. I can close my eyes and still see the patterns of our brown rug. Sometimes, I was washing the floors of the veranda—for some reason we called it the hallway. I would wash the mud spots from under black shoes, lifting them all, one pair at a time, wiping out autumn mud spots, then melted snow puddles, then spring slush spots. If I close my eyes, I can still see the small blue squares of tile installed by my father's hands.

I dreamed about a day when our whole street—no, our whole city—would see this miraculous healing, and everyone would get saved. Many years later, I realized that this was simple childlike faith in its purest form. I didn't just hope for Anton's healing, I was sure that it would come. I absolutely knew that God would heal him. This was the one and only possible option.

All we needed to do was just wait for the miracle.

First, Anton had lost his sight in one eye. Then when he was two years old, he became completely blind. He would recognize everyone in our family, and even our frequent guests, by our voices. Then when he stopped walking and became bedridden, he could recognize people by the sound their footsteps made in the hall. We all remember our old set of wooden colored pencils. There were only six or eight of them in all, and to us kids it seemed to be almost magical that he could tell their color just by touching them. Adults understood; the loss of vision had sharpened his other senses.

My older brother was learning how to play the piano, and he would play all the songs we sang at church, as well as some others, "by ear." Antoshka knew many of them by heart, but this one was his favorite:

> *Everyone, rejoice with me;*
> *There's no doubt that I am saved.*
> *Even if the whole world contradicts me,*
> *I know that I am saved in Christ.*

I still do not know who wrote that song, and I have never heard it anywhere else, except back in my childhood. Last year, my older brother flew in from Russia to visit us. I was preparing dinner for both of our families. While I was setting the table, he sat at our piano in the dining room and began to tickle my nerves with the melodies from our childhood. All seven of our kids were actively getting to know each other.

Just then, as I carried another dish from the kitchen to the dining room table, my heart sank. Suddenly I was out of breath from the wave of emotions that came over me. "Everyone, rejoice with me…" He was playing that very song. I froze in the doorway and begged him, "Please, Sergei, please stop, stop playing! *Stop!* I can't bear to hear it any longer!"

Time is a powerful anesthetic, but it does not dull this kind of pain.

A few months before our baby sister, Anechka, was born, Mom and I went to a specialty store. It was a grocery store for war veterans and *mnogodetnie* families[1]. There, parents could buy things

---

[1] *Mnogodetnie.* Literally translated "with many children." In the former USSR, large families were categorized as "needy" and were allowed certain privileges, such as being able to purchase food at government distribution centers that were closed to the general public. Although the monthly family allowance was miniscule in today's equivalent, this provided much needed support for people struggling to survive amid economic collapse and widespread food shortages.

that were not available to the general public—cheese, bologna, buckwheat grain. Our allowance was one kilogram per month for six people. But this was still back in Soviet times, way before humanitarian aid and the beginnings of perestroika[2]. We were profoundly grateful.

This shopping trip was one of those rare moments when Mom and I got to go out of the house together. After we got the groceries, I begged her to go to the nearby *Detsky Mir*[3]. Those of us who are ex-Soviet citizens over forty will be able to understand the vocabulary of that era: *golyye polki*—"bare shelves"; *vibrosili*—"thrown out"; *dostali*—"got me some." Back then, most of what we buy today would have been categorized as "deficit"[4]— product shortage—items.

We walked along through the half-empty store with weak hope. Suddenly I spotted a white shirt with black buttons in the children's section. And I could not understand why my mom was hesitant on buying it for Anton.

---

[2] *Perestroika* translated from Russian is "restructuring." A Soviet political movement aimed on restructuring the collapsing economy that permitted private ownership of businesses.

[3] *Detsky Mir* translates as "Children's World," the largest Soviet chain department store dedicated to children. In theory, parents could buy everything from baby items to kid's bikes. In practice, at the time the author is describing these events, it was mostly empty of merchandise, because of impending economic collapse.

[4] "Deficit" referred to widespread product shortages, a disastrous result of the Soviet planned economy, a constant shortage of certain goods and services.

She tried to explain. "My dear, our Antoshka never goes anywhere. He is in bed all the time, and for him the soft flannel shirts are more comfortable."

"But Mom, after all, the Lord will heal Anton very soon, and he has nothing at all to wear to church!" I remember in great detail how I was trying to convince my mom to buy it. And my mother bought the shirt.

Perhaps the adults understood that Anton was losing his strength and dying. Even though I was helping to care for him and saw how the tumor was growing larger and larger, he no longer wanted anyone except his mom. So we just helped change the cloth under his huge, hideous, foul-smelling, bleeding wound that resembled a second head. He was dying, but I still couldn't put it all together.

Only when my mother began to have contractions did Dad begin to take care of Antoshka. A week after giving birth, Mom came back, replacing Dad, who was visibly cast down and thinner.

Mom's milk dried up almost immediately. Thank God, Anechka was a very calm baby. Her bassinet was placed into our parents' bedroom, and Antoshka was moved to the unfolded sofa in the living room.

I turned eleven in December.

January 13 fell on a cold, snowy Tuesday. I came home from school; my dad was in the garage. I said the usual hello and was about to go into the house, but he stopped me.

"Honey, I need to tell you something…"

Our memories have an amazing capacity to store not only the dates and facts but also miniscule details such as tone of voice, aromas, colors, and emotions—emotions that never dull regardless of time passed.

I'm writing this after thirty years, yet it seems like I'm still there, shivering from the cold. I can still smell gasoline and some kind of engine oil from behind the wide open garage door, and in response to my curious glance, I hear my father speak with an unrecognizable voice, "Our Antoshka has died." Darkness.

Then the sound of my echoing screams, "No, this can't be true, no, no, *no!* God promised He would heal him. No!"

Then I am inside the house. It is very quiet; everyone is whispering. I shiver from the cold, a coldness I never felt before—the coldness of death. This very morning in the same room, my mom and I turned Antoshka from one side to the other right before school. We did this as a team, one holding his head and the other, his limp body. One, two, three—we turned him gently and carefully. Only eight hours ago.

Antoshka lies still, his hair neatly combed, and he is wearing the new white shirt with black buttons. That very same shirt I picked out for him.

Mom is not screaming; humility is imprinted on her face even in her grief. Just three months after giving birth. Many months practically without sleep. How did she cope? How would she survive this? Where would she find answers to all her questions? How will she explain this to her children? How shall she explain this to herself? Does she now have not two, but only one son, and three daughters? No, she would never erase him from the total sum of her children. Except now, one of her boys is in heaven.

It is late into the night, but no one can sleep. I am sitting next to my grandfather—a pastor, an artist, and a sculptor. I'm watching him write a Scripture verse in beautiful gold letters; he is writing them on the lid of the coffin. The text from the Bible is from the Book of Revelation: "Blessed are the dead which die in the Lord."

> "Blessed are the dead which die in the Lord."

I slowly read the phrase "die in" aloud, and I ask my grandfather, "Shouldn't that phrase be written as 'die for'?"

Grandpa stops for a moment, gets out his Bible, and after checking the spelling, continues with his work.

Well, let it be "in," I thought. *Why are they blessed, though? Could it be because they no longer suffer in pain? How could being separated from everyone and everything you love be a blessing?*

That January was bitterly cold. The road to the cemetery up on the hill behind the residential neighborhood was very long, first on foot along the road, then in the back of an open dump truck. Someone was saying something about how wonderful Anton must feel being in heaven with Jesus. Just before they closed the lid of the coffin, Dad came up and put both of his hands on Anton's little body, and for a moment I thought he was going to pick him up, hug him tight, and Anton would come back to life.

Then, for some reason, my older brother and I stood on our knees right at the edge of the frozen dirt mound. Blue coffin, red carnations all around the jagged, ugly, deep hole. Then, the bloodcurdling sound of the hammer, pounding long nails into its lid.

And that is all.

* * *

The first years after Anton's death were filled with worry about our dad: frequent heart problems, his state of impending heart attack, frequent hospitalizations. Mom would wake me and my brother in the middle of the night, and we would run to wake our friends who lived on the next street over. They had a telephone, and we would beg them to call for an ambulance. Then we waited at our gate for an ambulance to come to us. Those long minutes of waiting would seem like an unending nightmare. Once, I grabbed onto the arm of a half-asleep paramedic, and I literally dragged him into the house pleading, "Please hurry! Please help my dad!"

But what about Mom? How did she survive this? Who supported her? Who helped her? Never in my life did I hear anyone describe her as a strong woman or a bright soul. She was quiet and humble. She did not demand attention to herself. Mom rarely complained about anything, and she would often pray, pouring her heart out in tears. Not once did she say anything against God.

would often pray, pouring her heart out in tears. Not once did she say anything against God. It seemed as if she always loved him, accepting His love and passing it unto us.

Two years after Anechka's birth, Mom gave birth to Irochka. After two more years, Nastya, and after three more, Alex. Two sons and five daughters. And one in heaven. Every day she would wake up to live this day for others. She did not retreat into her own pain, nor did she wear it as a badge of courage. Moreover, she did not seek pity. Her self-sacrificing life was described best in her own words: "I have to live for my other children. I have to rejoice with them, for them, and for their own sake."

Almost twenty years later, I also became a mother. And I suddenly realized the weight of suffering that had fallen on my mother. I wondered how she was able to bear it all. Now I know for myself what it means to be pregnant with a child, to feel his first kicks, to rub my own growing belly, to dream about him, hoping to God that it will all be okay. Then to give birth and to fall in love with him at first sight. No, honestly, it must be the father who falls in love at first sight with his child. We mothers love our child from the womb with unrelenting love that lasts forever.

How unbearable it must be to see your child suffer, knowing that you cannot help him, and then watch him suffer and die. How do you survive something like this?

How do you survive something like this? Perhaps only through being strengthened by faith.

Where do you draw your strength from? How can you then carry and bear more children, sewing new lace baby bonnets and swaddling clothes for them, sewing new skirts for your girls from your own old ones? How can this be possible? Perhaps only through being strengthened by faith.

I've told you already that Faith-Hope-Love would have fit my Mom better than just Hope—Nadezhda.

Her faith in God is not just a factual recognition of his existence. Perhaps not knowing all the theological terms, Mom always believed in his sovereignty and his omnipresence; she knew he is all-knowing and almighty. By living out her faith, she had developed a genuine trust in God.

Mom just turned sixty-three. She looks great; she continues being active, even more positive, and always joyful. After a decade of living apart, we now live on the same continent and even in the same country with my parents; our homes are only a few miles apart.

Over the years, Mom has improved her culinary technique to a mastery level, and for that reason, my children just love to visit Grandma. She bakes us homemade bread and delicious dumplings, pierogis, and cabbage rolls that are all out of this world.

Her vegetable garden that fed our family back in the day with potatoes, tomatoes, and cucumbers is now a distant memory. Today her entire yard, both front and back, is planted with fragrant flowers. Her positivity and love extends even to her plants; it seems that flowers can't help but bloom all around her.

> Having endured many trials and heartaches in her life, Mom not only kept her faith but she was also able to pass it on to us. Now she is passing it on to our children.

And while my children eat all her delicious goodies, Mom pours me a cup of coffee, and I wait for her to sit next to me so that she can begin to do what only a few can—patiently listen to me. She listens attentively and with understanding, and yes, she always has something to say. But she does it when the moment is right. Her words are always filled with faith. "A gentle instruction is on her tongue" (Proverbs 31:26) is about her.

Having endured many trials and heartaches in her life, Mom not only kept her faith but she was also able to pass it on to us. Now she is passing it on to our children.

• LIFE LESSONS •

ABOUT GOD. God's sovereignty is not just another concept in a long list of attributes of God. His sovereignty is as real as His omnipresence and goodness. God is not Santa Claus; He is not a magician, granting our wishes and filling our orders on bettering our comfort levels in this life. God is the King of kings and the Lord of lords. God creates that what He Himself wills. And in turn He offers for us to believe and trust that **"all things work together for the good of those who love God: those who are called according to his purpose" (Romans 8:28 HCSB).**

ABOUT SUFFERING. Sometimes, when we stop focusing all our attention on our own suffering, our deepest wounds become less inflamed and less painful. We stop burying ourselves in our own hurts. When we live for others, we lay down ourselves and pour out our souls. Then in hindsight we stand in wonder, How did we manage to live through that torment? Pain and suffering are parts of our human existence, but it won't be so for long.
"'He will wipe every tear from their eyes. There will be no more death' or mourning or crying or pain, for the old order of things has passed away" (Revelation 21:4 NIV).

ABOUT LIFE. Surely at our present moment it may be completely incomprehensible how and why this or that event happened in our lives, but in God's master plan, this must have taken place. There will always be unanswered questions in this life. Because now we are looking as if through a dim glass lens, not only at the truths of Scripture and the deep secrets of our universe but also at our own lives. But there will be a time when every piece of the puzzle will fall into place, and we will have no more questions. This will take place beyond the threshold of death when we will look down at our earthly life from a heavenly perspective. **"For now we see only a reflection as in a mirror; then we shall see face to face. Now I know in part; then I shall know fully, even as I am fully known" (1 Corinthians 13:12 NIV).**

ABOUT FAITH. What can destroy my faith? What makes it grow stronger or weaker?

"But I was believing!" we sometimes cry with disappointment, wondering why we did not receive an answer to our prayer. Our faith in God must be greater than our faith in receiving some benefit from Him. In Hebrews 11:13 (NIV), we read, **"All these people were still living by faith when they died. They did not receive the things promised; they only saw them and welcomed them from a distance, admitting that they were foreigners and strangers on earth."** They did not receive what they were promised, but they did not die in disappointment; they died with faith in God!

ABOUT US. The hard blows of life can either break us or make us stronger. If we give up and let them, they can knock us down, press us to the ground, and trample us under. But there is always a chance for us to rise up again because the supernatural power of the Living God resides within us, the God Who mourns with those who mourn and **"gives strength to the weary and increases the power of the weak." (Isaiah 40:29 NIV).**

2

JOCHEBED.
VICTORY OF THE SLAVES

Early Saturday morning, three young girls arrived at Tushino airfield near Moscow where a flight club had just opened and the list of services included a new fad—skydiving. I'm not sure that I would have dared to jump if I had been married with children, but back then, nothing was holding me back. Being surrounded by good company, my sister Vera and my friend Larisa, also helped me overcome my fears.

There were about twenty of us. For most of us this was our first jump. Instructors deemed us capable of memorizing all the details instantly, word for word

> Overcoming yourself is one of the hardest victories to achieve, but it opens a pathway to so many others.

and on the fly, which meant they did not trouble us with long and boring preparations.

I remembered only one thing: If you don't want your legs to be broken, you need to keep them together and bent at the knees when landing. As a result, my legs remained intact, but obviously I forgot another part of the instruction where they said to pull down the lower lines after landing. My parachute, fast blown by the wind, dragged me across the field, giving my legs scrapes and bruises for keepsakes.

But it wasn't the landing that proved to be most terrifying in this whole experience.

I ponder the photograph taken there: all of us standing by a helicopter, wearing funny multicolored helmets. I, of course, am wearing the red one as red is my favorite color. No, we were not issued any kind of flight suits, which made us look a bit goofy.

With our bodies tightly strapped by belts and wearing all the equipment, we walked up to the helicopter. We were the only girls in that large group of men and guys, and at that moment we were still smiling and giggling. But when the helicopter gained altitude, the giant side door opened with a terrible roar; bright light and cold air rushed into the darkness of its metal belly.

The next few moments happened so fast, but as I was approaching the gaping wide door, I felt as if time had slowed down and I encountered my moment of realization. Thoughts rushed through my head with an incredible speed and shouting over the noise generated by helicopter blades, I tried to repeat them out loud. "I am no longer sure that I want to jump." But it seemed no one could hear me. Instructors began lining us up for the jump. We stood in a line. A heavy-set man, who probably did this hundreds or thousands of times, would put his massive hand on the shoulder of another thrill seeker, and every few seconds, with a thundering "Go!" he would push them out into the vast emptiness.

Honestly, even now if I close my eyes, I can still picture small squares of fields, a thinning ribbon of the river, a patch of woods, and the residential neighborhoods in the distance. I see it all from high above, from a bird's-eye perspective. My feet become wobbly, I am nauseated, and I feel like sitting down.

"Maybe they can still take me back down to the ground?"

"Please?"

I take a look back at the girls, peering into their eyes, then a man standing in front of me takes a step forward, or rather downward, and by doing so he frees the spot in the doorway for me. I take my last few steps forward, my legs stiff and shaky, then I feel that strong hand on my own shoulder, I hear "Go!"

And, horrified, I step right into thin air.

I fall like a stone for the first three seconds. Here it is, the feeling of free fall! Believe you me, these seconds were enough; they were unforgettable.

> Horrified, I step right into thin air.

But then when the parachute fully opens, euphoria sets in. The quiet is extraordinary. I feel indescribable exuberance. Finally I realize that my parachute is tightly strapped to me, and there is no need for me to be clinching the straps so tightly. I open my fists, freeing my fingers, white from tension. I spread my arms wide, and then I want to scream and sing and cry all at the same time—I am alone up here in the sky; I am flying!

This is how volatile my emotions can be. On board that helicopter, I was absolutely terrified of the uncertainty, but then, I was flying—midair, experiencing pure joy and happiness.

I think I gained a valuable insight through this experience of flight, paired with the thrill of victory over myself and my fear.

Surely, jumping with a parachute is just a thrill and completely unnecessary in the grand scheme of life. But I'm not talking about that. I'm talking about overcoming yourself—because it happens to be an essential skill and a vital necessity.

> Challenges can arise suddenly and without warning ... you will need to take a step forward and leap into the unknown.

Challenges can arise suddenly and without warning, situations in which you will need to take a step forward and leap into the unknown. But this skill is acquired by taking small strides through miniscule, everyday little victories. We all know that victory over ourselves can manifest in simply fasting every Wednesday or in restraining our own flow of words that offend or complain or even in saying no to dessert. As I understand it, overcoming yourself is one of the hardest victories to achieve, but it opens a pathway to so many others.

One of the best known biblical accounts is the story of Moses. He is one of the brightest characters of the Old Testament, humanity's first legislator. But behind every great man stands a woman of no lesser greatness. It is undoubtedly true, and in this case, it was his mother!

Jochebed was a great woman of faith who obtained many spiritual victories in her life. She was entrusted by God to give birth and to raise three children, each of whom played a major part in history. Miriam, her eldest child, was a bold soul; she was strong-willed and operated in prophetic and poetic gifts. Aaron was the father of the priesthood. He was also speaking for Moses in negotiations with Pharaoh. Moses was the deliverer, the first legislator in the history of mankind, a strong leader, an advocate for his people, and a close friend of God Himself.

When we read the Book of Exodus, in the beginning of the story of Moses, the name of his mother is not even mentioned. It simply calls her *wife* or *woman*, depending on the translation. It is not until the list of genealogies in the sixth chapter of Genesis (v. 20) and in the Book of Numbers (26:59) that we learn her name: "Amram's wife—Jochebed—daughter of Levi." She bore three children to Amram: Aaron, Miriam, and Moses. Her life cannot be described as extraordinary, but at the same time it was remarkable. Jochebed lived in difficult times in a foreign country where all the Jews were enslaved, with all the ensuing consequences of slavery. Even though she was a slave, it was up to Jochebed to determine whether or not she would trust in God or obey Pharaoh's laws. Not only was she a wife and a mother, but she was a woman who knew the Living God. Overcoming herself was no easy task, but she remained unrelenting, facing horrifying circumstances and her own fears.

Let's take a closer look at five of her most important victories.

Overcoming Fear

As Jochebed learns that she will become a mother for the third time, mixed feelings flood her soul. She already has a twelve-year-old daughter and a three-year-old son. It seems that this time, there should be no preference for the baby's gender. But from the moment she realized she was pregnant, she does not cease to pray, *Anything except a son, God! Please Lord, not a boy! Let it be a girl.*

She is living in Egypt—a prosperous civilization that had reached the peak of its development, where new cities rise out of the sands, enormous pyramids are being built, with the exception of Goshen, which is overpopulated with Jewish slaves. In Goshen, parents tell their children bedtime stories about Abraham, Isaac, and Jacob; they tell stories about Joseph and the chosen people of the Most High God; of how they all came to live in Egypt. These stories raise many questions. *Are you sure that he was second after Pharaoh? Can it all be true or is it just a myth?* Everything looks so different now. The scars from the lashes laid by Egyptian managers heal slowly on the sunburned backs of their slaves, but the daily demand of brick production is still barely accomplishable. The slaves are on the verge of rebellion, and they cry out to their God.

Concerned about the state of his affairs, Pharaoh had become desperate to reduce his male slave population without limiting his own demands for construction. He needed his Jews as slave laborers, not as young warriors. When the birth control plan that had been implemented with the help of the local midwives had failed, the matter had been put into the hands of the Egyptian soldiers.

> Pharaoh had become desperate to reduce his male slave population without limiting his own demands for construction. He needed his Jews as slave laborers, not as young warriors.

Then, the groans of the enslaved men had grown silent; you could only hear the sobs of pregnant women gripped in fear and the bloodcurdling screams of mothers as their newborn sons were ripped from their arms.

They did not think slavery could become any more horrifying!

The Nile, the beautiful river that fed them with fish, had become a burial ground for their newborn sons.

After nine months of struggling with her fear, Jochebed gives birth to a healthy baby. Terrified, she

> Terrified, she dares not to ask because she knows it would mean the difference between life and death.

dares not to ask *Is it a daughter or a son?* because she knows it would mean the difference between life and death.

Nevertheless, she sees the answer written in the eyes of her midwife, a look of sympathy and regret. Now, it is only a matter of time. In densely populated Goshen, everyone knows how this will end. The odds of hiding a newborn baby seem impossible; Pharaoh's spies are all around, ready to give away any family hiding a male child for a small reward.

This mother takes her son into her arms, looks at his tiny face, and then suddenly she sees something. Of course, the child is beautiful! But underneath clumpy black curls, brown eyes, and a cute distinct nose, something else is revealed to her—her son's great destiny and faith in the greatness of her God.

Jochebed and Amram look at each other; their eyes meet and they are no longer afraid. Now they have a firm confidence and trust in God's protection. *We will not give up our son!* Faith replaces fear; this explains why Moses was hidden for three months!

In the book of Hebrews, there is a chapter devoted to the heroes of the faith. And it tells their story: "By faith Moses's parents hid him for three months after he was born, because they saw he was no ordinary child, and they were not afraid of the king's command" (11:23 NIV).

Overcoming Circumstances

Three months go by. It has become impossible for Jochebed to hide her baby any longer. Soldiers could arrive at any moment.

What to do? Who can I ask for advice? Where can I look for help? No one has been in my situation before. She thinks long and hard. She prays and she decides to save her child.

You, my dear reader, might be right in the midst of similar circumstances. Know this, when a life-affirming thought comes to you, you must run with it. This is God talking to your heart, the same way He did with Jochebed.

> When a life-affirming thought comes to you, you must run with it. This is God talking to your heart.

This mother weaved a basket with her own hands while her chubby-cheeked baby peacefully slept next to her. She sized it up to make sure it would fit him comfortably. But the peaceful silence of the room must have been no match to the raging storm thundering in her head, her thoughts of fear.

I must be crazy; he will surely drown! The Nile is infested with crocodiles! They will catch me on the way to the river! It would have been easier to lose him when he was just born! I won't let him go! Jochebed touches his soft cheek and whispers words of faith, "My beautiful boy. Divine destiny.

"Our almighty God!"

She wraps her baby boy in a blanket and lays him in that tar-soaked basket, and together with Miriam carries him to the river, where she sets him afloat into the waters of the Nile.

And what happens next is like a magical fairy tale: There was a real princess and a cute Jewish girl who, by the way, just happened to be nearby and offered to find a wet nurse for the child.

This truly was a miraculous deliverance! As it turns out, angels can shut the mouths of crocodiles just the same as those of the lions. Once again Jochebed holds her baby in her arms, but now she is nursing the adopted son of Pharaoh's daughter, and she keeps whispering, "My beautiful boy. Divine destiny. Our almighty God!"

Overcoming Yourself

Five years flew by way too fast. Yes, she was so grateful she had the opportunity to nurture and raise her own son. She was there when he had his first teeth, when he took the first steps, and when he said his first words. Those who loved him were all there. His mother was able to instill in him her love for God and love for his people, and even though this love will grow cold for a while, it will reawaken just in time for the great exodus. Still, the dreadful hour of separation was fast approaching as her boy was growing older. God only knows how many times Jochebed secretly hoped that no one would come for him, that the princess had forgotten all about the boy and the whole adoption story only happened so that he could be saved from certain death. *If only* she *knew that it was exactly that!*

Only, the plan of salvation was much grander—it included not only her Moses but also hundreds of thousands of his people.

In order to let go of her son, to let him be taken to the palace, Jochebed desperately needed to overcome herself—she needed to have victory over her own desires. She had to humble herself and trust in God until she could say the same words that Mary would repeat when facing uncertainty, "I am the servant of the Lord. Be it unto me according to Thy word" (Luke 1:38, paraphrased).

> Jochebed desperately needed to overcome herself—she needed to have victory over her own desires. She had to humble herself and trust in God.

Waiting for the fulfillment of God's promises, though, was not easy. She waited for forty long years. During that time Moses was enjoying a luxurious palace lifestyle and getting brilliantly educated. While he was proudly overlooking grand cities and pyramids and making plans for his bright future, all his mother could do during this time was to continue to pray for him.

Victory over Defeat

Her heart must have leaped with joy when she heard, "Moses is back!"

I knew it; I always knew he would return to help us. God has heard our prayers, our redemption is near!

God had always heard their cries and prayers, but Moses was not yet ready to lead his people out of slavery. The desert, where he had to walk for another forty years, was a trial for his mother as well as for Moses.

And instead of the long-awaited deliverance, the answer to Jochebed's forty-year-long prayer felt like a catastrophic disaster. "This must be some kind of mistake," she cried. "It just cannot be true! Why is Pharaoh looking for Moses? They are looking to kill him?" This time, Moses had to run for his own life. Her heart sank. *Where could he go? Could he ever come back?*

Her long-awaited boy, the son of Amram and Jochebed, lost everything in a blink of an eye. Not only did he lose his royal privilege; moreover, he lost the faith of his Jewish brothers in him.

For the next forty years, his mother didn't hear anything about him. Yet, the mother's love is unrelenting. Jochebed remained steadfast in the face of uncertainty. And her prayers would keep sustaining him even there in the desert as she continued to whisper and pray, "My beautiful boy. Divine destiny. Our almighty God!"

Perhaps Jochebed never saw Moses again; maybe she did not live long enough to see the day when he returned to bring them out of slavery. But she did not relent. They all waited for him—his mother, his father, Aaron, and Miriam. And while Moses was undergoing his spiritual desert experience in preparation to fulfill his mission, his mother's faith made evident the things they all hoped for. Her faith stood victorious over despair.

> Jochebed remained steadfast in the face of uncertainty. And her prayers would keep sustaining him.

Inherited Victory

Heredity is something more than just your eye color, your height, or the shape of your nose. Other characteristics can be passed on as well, such as tenacity, strength of character, and willpower.

It could be that Moses soaked up these qualities with his mother's milk, character traits that helped him become a true leader and the good shepherd for his people. He would stand his ground and would never give up. He was relentless in his mission—never looking back.

Many things happened during the next forty years while millions of freed slaves, none of whom yet knew what to do with their newfound freedom, were wandering in the desert. They would often betray God, who saved them, as well as Moses, who devoted his life to caring for them. The lack of simple necessities like food, water, and heat, not to mention being constantly on the move at a moment's notice, gave the people plenty of reasons for grumbling and complaining. But Moses possessed superhuman-like strength to constantly deal with millions of ungrateful Jews, and it is not surprising that the Bible calls him the humblest man on earth (see Numbers 12:3).

One unbelievable episode is described in the thirty-second chapter of Exodus.

Moses was standing on top of the mountain, communicating with God. There, God Himself gave him the Ten Commandments. It is truly the most remarkable moment in human history. Their encounter began with God proclaiming that He alone shall be their God, and He shall make these miserable people into "the kingdom of priests and the holy nation" (Exodus 19:4–6). Besides the Ten Commandments, God gave them rules and instructions on how they shall now live: how to build the sanctuary, how they should worship, how they should behave, as well as their sanitary practices and relational boundaries. God, who loved them, took care of every single detail. Just as an eagle teaches its eaglets to fly, God prepared his children for their new life as free people. He Himself told Moses, "I carried you on eagle's wings and brought you to myself" (Exodus 19:4). They thought that God helped them escape from their enemy and oppression, but deliverance was only part of His plan—rather, the Lord drew them to Himself because the Father always longs for fellowship with His children.

Then comes something completely unexpected, a twist in this story.

We read that the whole mountain was shrouded in clouds and darkness because the Lord came down on it in fire, and smoke rose from the mountain. Up there, Moses was communing with God while the people waited at the base of the mountain. But soon they grew tired of waiting. Some no longer believed that he was still alive; others doubted that he would ever return to them.

People gathered around Aaron, now the high priest, saying, "Come, make us a god who will go before us. As for this fellow, Moses, who brought us out of Egypt, we do not know what has happened to him" (Exodus 19:1). They actually said fellow. What? Had they suddenly forgotten who Moses was? Had they forgotten his God? Seriously? Have they forgotten the locusts, the frogs, the gnats, the total darkness, the golf ball-sized hail, and the death of the Egyptian firstborn? Did all the plagues of Egypt no longer stir their memories? And what of the nightmarish walk along the bottom of the Red Sea amid the liquid walls of the water? They asked Aaron to make them another god. Make him from what? From trinkets like earrings and rings? Did they really think that an idol could lead them? That it would have the same ability to provide for them and bring them into the promised land—the land flowing with milk and honey?

It's not hard to understand God's reaction—why God urged Moses to come down from the mountain. "Now leave me alone so my fierce anger can blaze against them, and I will destroy them. Then I will make you, Moses, into a great nation" (Exodus 32:10 NLT).

Most of us would have said *Amen!* to this proposal, but not Moses. To him this unprecedented exodus from Egypt was just the beginning. *It simply cannot end here, not like this!* The heart of this eighty-year-old man was set on completing his mission. He never let go of hope, never gave up, and never lost faith. Even to the point of disagreeing with God Himself!

How dare he argue with the Lord? God knows what is best, right? But Moses was not accustomed to surrendering lightly, and he dared to step in between God's wrath and the people. In that moment, Moses had just become an intercessor for his people.

He began to beg God and even dared to remind the Lord of His own promises to Abraham, Isaac, and Jacob. Finally, Moses was granted his request. "The Lord turned from the evil which He had thought to do to His people" (32:14 NKJV).

The victory of the spirited old man was made possible partly because of his mother, because from infancy she had taught him to never give up, never lose heart, and never fall victim to circumstance. In truth, this was Jochebed's victory as well, only it became evident in the life of her son Moses, who inherited her strong spirit, unrelenting faith, and tender love for his people.

• LIFE LESSONS •

ABOUT GOD. God loves people. As we read the Bible, we discover that it was Moses who was the first person to learn something of God's character from God Himself. And because the Lord remains the same "yesterday, today, and forever" (Hebrews 13:8), we know these words speak of His favor toward us as well: **The Lord, the Lord, the compassionate and gracious God, slow to anger, abounding in love and faithfulness, maintaining love to thousands, and forgiving wickedness, rebellion and sin." (Exodus 34:6–7)**

ABOUT US. Overcoming ourselves is the greatest of victories, even though it is not easy to entrust ourselves to God, especially if we lack reasons for our circumstances. But, "we know that in all things God works for the good of those who love him, who have been called according to his purpose" (Romans 8:28).

ABOUT LIFE. Adversity is a call to action. It is a way to become an overcomer. Simply waiting for things to change is the fate of victims who are mauled by their circumstances. God, who is always in control of our life events, is waiting for us to step into action with Him and to take our own steps of faith.
Yet, he did not waver through unbelief regarding the promise of God, but was strengthened in his faith and gave glory to God, being fully persuaded that God had power to do what he had promised. (Romans 4:20–21)

ABOUT DEFEAT. Being defeated in one battle does not mean that you will surely lose the war. In the end, even when facing defeat, the final victory is given to the one who won't relent. This happened to King David. One time as he returned from battlefield, he was greeted by the ashes of a completely burned down and devastated city—Sekelag. His men wept and mourned for their wives, sons, and daughters taken captive by the enemy. This total disaster could have led to an even worse tragedy.

Then came the turning point; it always comes when we turn our eyes from our own pain to God and begin seeking His counsel, looking for help from the Lord. This is exactly what David did. We can follow his example, even if we lose our own "city—Sekelag": **David was greatly distressed because the men were talking of stoning him; each one was bitter in spirit because of his sons and daughters. But David found strength in the Lord his God ...and David inquired of the Lord ...David recovered everything the Amalekites had taken. (1 Samuel 30:6, 8, 18).** This was a post-defeat victory.

ABOUT FEAR. Faith overcomes fear. God Himself is impressed by our faith, and in response, certain things and actions begin to produce evidence of what we had hoped for.
More often than not, reality and facts dictate to us what we ought to believe. The factual statistics can shout over and drown out words of faith. Therefore, the apostle Paul reminds us, "For we walk by faith, and not by sight" (2 Corinthians 5:7 NKJV) and "Faith is by hearing, and hearing by the Word of God" (Romans 10:17).

3

HANNAH.
TIT FOR TAT

A few years ago, I had a unique piece of jewelry. I wore it all year long, every day, without ever taking it off; it was an incredibly valuable piece. No, it was not made of platinum or gold or even silver; it was a thin, simple, white-metal chain with a beautiful heart pendant. Honestly, this was the cheapest piece of jewelry my family ever gave me as a gift. The little heart on a chain was presented to me with its price tag still attached—$5.99.

This period of my life was unforgettable, and I am starting to miss it already. Back then we had three little kids who were always with me.

I don't exactly remember why I went to the store on that particular day. T.J.Maxx is one of my favorite stores; you can buy everything except groceries there: dishes, bed linens, clothes, shoes, toys, jewelry, and perfume—it's all there. When it comes to shopping, my son, Paul, is just like his father; he absolutely detests shopping. So during these forced trips to the store, he mostly sat in a shopping cart with a book. But on the other hand, my girls are the exact opposite. They are always happy to help me find what I need, and even that which I don't, but apparently they must have.

While I was busy looking for what I came for, the girls were nearby. Then, I noticed that they were cheerfully whispering to each other while hiding something in their hands. I got a bit suspicious but continued to watch them from behind. Usually, if they wanted to buy something for themselves or for someone else, they would openly bring it to me and show what they wanted to buy. A bad feeling crept over me, but I immediately dismissed it. I've described theft to them in vivid details. They knew that God sees everything and what stealing was. They also knew that there were cameras in every store.

But then they both came up to me, grinning from ear to ear. I could see the excitement in their eyes; they were absolutely thrilled about their great idea. "Mommy, please give us some money. It's a secret, but we really need to buy something!"

At that point Paul put his book aside, and the three of them whispered together. I pretended not to hear anything. I tried not to notice a box with a price tag oddly hanging from it and held by a tiny hand. Back then, our kids didn't have any money of their own. They usually got Lego and dolls for their birthdays. Well, I thought, if Paul, my very pragmatic boy, likes their idea, then I guess they can purchase it by themselves, so I opened my wallet and handed them a $20 bill.

As the kids went up to the register, the cashier gave me a questioning look. I nodded back with full approval, watching them from at a distance. Little Ariana, on her tiptoes and with both hands on the counter, was actively participating in the whole process. The cashier tried handing the box back to them, but they asked for a plastic bag and carefully wrapped the gift in it. When we finished our shopping, as I intentionally kept their anticipation high by my ridiculous guessing game—*What could it be? Who is it for?*—the kids were beyond excited.

When we finally got home, they waited patiently for Dad to come home, and then, with full sincerity they presented me with this gift. Not in honor of any specific day nor for any reason, they simply gave me a token of their love on that cold fall Tuesday. Needless to say, I was so touched. And when my husband asked the kids where they got the money for their mother's present, they plainly said, "We asked Mom for it!"

Perhaps more pragmatic parents would think of this whole thing as foolishness, and they would explain to their child that if you did not pay for it yourself, then this cannot be a real gift. Asking for something from someone with one intention—to give it back? Perhaps this is a childish thing, or maybe, this can only be normal for truly humble people.

"Mom, give me some money, I will buy you a gift with it!" is not an absurdity. It is passionate heartfelt love.

I absolutely love real-life stories of ordinary people, stories told without colorful embellishments, simply recorded as they truly happened. We learn the most from everyday heroes because we can recognize ourselves in their stories, and in some way we want to be just like them. Perhaps that is why we all love Bible stories so much, and sometimes it is the person's flaws that most attract our attention. Here is one such story, a story of a woman who asked God for a present that she herself would later bring back as a gift unto the Lord.

> We learn the most from everyday heroes because we can recognize ourselves in their stories, and in some way we want to be just like them.

The first precondition for a woman's happiness is love and a happy marriage. The second is children. The second should not come without the first. The first can be ruined by the absence of the second.

This story is 3,000 years old, yet it holds a timeless narrative: love and drama, pain and happiness. It is the account of one ordinary family in the newly liberated nation of Israel. Just 300 years before, Jews

> This story is 3,000 years old, yet it holds a timeless narrative: love and drama, pain and happiness.

had been slaves in Egypt, but now they live in the cities and villages on the fertile plains in the land of God's promise, flowing with milk and honey.

Hannah has been very fortunate to marry a good man—a minister, a Levite from the tribe of Ephraim. He tenderly loves and adores Hannah. And like all newlyweds, they eagerly wait to have children—a blessing from the Lord.

Years go by, but there are no children. Hannah hopes and prays, yet every month she is disappointed, again and again. Every month she sheds bitter tears. Hannah dreads talking to her husband Elkanah about this because she knows the traditional way of dealing with infertility. She also knows that he needs children, children who will continue his lineage and be his heirs and helpers in family business.

Back then, if a wife was unable to bear children, the husband would take another wife. Sometimes, a desperate women would give her own maidservant to her husband as a concubine to avoid conflicts of rivalry with a new wife. It is no secret how difficult it would be for two women to get along in the same kitchen, yet alone in the same bedroom—even worse in the heart of the same man.

Hannah's fears are well founded, and instead of the long-awaited baby, the newest member of their family becomes Peninnah—her husband's second wife. Soon long-awaited sons and daughters are born for Elkanah by Peninnah. And it seems that all should now be well. Hannah is still loved by her devoted husband, and now her husband had children.

But Peninnah knew that Elkanah loved his first wife more than her, which made her own happiness impossible.

Even with Hannah's husband's full devotion, even as Elkanah loudly proclaims that he is better for her than ten sons, Hannah continues to suffer because she wants a child so much. As it turns out, having a husband and having a child are not one and the same. One woman had love—without children; the other had children—without love. What a twisted love triangle from the Old Testament.

Elkanah is a devout Levite, so every year he takes his whole family on pilgrimage. They go to worship the Lord of Hosts in Shiloh. It will take another 100 years for the magnificent Temple of God to be built by King Solomon, but for now, everyone travels to worship at Shiloh, because God's presence abides in that place. The sanctuary also serves as a home for Eli. The old God-fearing man serves the Lord as High Priest here, but his two sons are wicked men.

I feel like we must stop here and admire Elkanah's devotion.

These were desperate times for the sanctuary. Terrible rumors were going around about Eli's sons, Hophni and Phinehas. The young men completely disregarded the rituals of sacrifice and were utterly corrupt. All they were interested in was delicious food and pretty women, and all this lewd behavior happened right where people came to worship the Lord. This lawlessness literally turned people away from bringing their sacrifices. So, the truly devout Jews would avoid coming to celebrate at Shiloh, for they refused to support those who dishonor God by using their offerings, and they would rather disobey the Lord's command than to see utter depravity in the sanctuary.

By doing so, the righteous Jews who refused to support corruption and debauchery, in all actuality, deprived themselves of the opportunity to worship their own God. Surely Elkanah understood all this. Moreover, as a Levite he realized the gravity of a priesthood sin. But he also knew that he was bringing his offerings and sacrifices not to the priests, Hophni and Phinehas, and not even unto the righteous priest Eli, but unto the Lord God Himself. So he continued to come, year after year, as the Lord had commanded them through Moses. Perhaps Hannah herself saw the corruption perpetrated by the sons of Eli; maybe she thought, *If I had a son, I would raise him to serve the Lord. If only I had a son.*

A trip from Ramah to Shiloh is about eight and a half miles on foot Elkanah and the two women, with several young children in tow, walk beside a donkey loaded with baggage, followed by a few of their best sheep, intended for sacrifice.

They make this journey in fulfillment of God's commandment to bring offerings and to worship the Lord. It is a celebration for everyone—everyone except Hannah. Yes, of course she loves God; every year she comes to pray in the sanctuary with hope and antici-

> Year after year, she prays, each time kneeling a little bit lower, each time her voice a little bit quieter. With every passing year, Hannah's heart shatters deeper and deeper.

pation. Year after year, she prays, each time kneeling a little bit lower, each time her voice a little bit quieter. With every passing year and every new baby birthed by Peninnah, Hannah's heart shatters deeper and deeper, and her eyes shed a lot of tears.

Her rival is like an open sore causing years of pain and humiliation. Revenge is Peninnah's favorite punishment, all because her husband is in love with Hannah. But Hannah does not gossip, she does not complain, nor does she try to turn Elkanah against his second wife. Perhaps he doesn't even know how much pain, resentment, and utter hatred exists between his wives. Men usually notice facts and events rather than underhanded remarks, bitter sarcasm, or subtle hints. But things that may seem trivial to some can be a source of great distress to others.

It is time for the festive dinner after the sacrifice. Elkanah's whole family has been together for several days, counting their journey up to Shiloh and the length of the Festival. Many old friends and acquaintances are there too! Everyone admires the sons and daughters of Elkanah, mothered by Peninnah, noting how much the babies have grown by now.

And then they silently smile at Hannah. Everyone quietly pities her without any questions asked and seeing the proud look on Peninnah face, they pity her even more.

The sound of festive music, the smell of grilled meat and grateful cheers make this harvest dinner a joyful festival. These people worked hard; they sowed and plowed while praying for rain all year long. Now, having reaped a great harvest, they come to honor the Lord, who answered their prayers by blessing their hard work.

Joy must be easy for them, Hannah thinks. *They've received what they have prayed for.* And she begins to weep. The food, the wine, the children on her husband's lap, the music, the people, and the look of contempt on Peninnah's face while she is holding her new baby—Hannah is watching it all through the salty mist of her anguish as pain streams out of her soul and flows down her cheeks as bitter tears.

> Joy must be easy for them. They've received what they have prayed for.

Elkanah puts his arm around Hannah's shoulder as he holds a child on his knee. He wonders, *Why?*

Why can't he understand? Elkanah, you truly are a good husband, but a husband cannot substitute for children; it is not one and the same! Yes, I am so happy to be your wife, but at the same time, I am in anguish, because I cannot be a mother to your children. Hannah quietly holds back her tears and pushes her big plate aside, the one with double portions of all the best meat on it. She quietly gets up and slips away from the dinner festivities.

No, she doesn't blame anyone. Neither does she expect understanding from people.

But she has a hard time tolerating everyone's silent sympathy and blank pitiful stares: *Oh poor dear, what a terrible punishment this must be, or worse, maybe she is under some kind of curse.*

People can be so heartless and cruel, even out of compassion.

Hannah returns to the sanctuary. By now it is quiet and empty.

After the sacrifices have ceased, having done their duty, everyone has gone off to celebrate. On one hand, whispering prayers in a crowded sanctuary among the noise felt easier. On the other hand, now she is alone in here, and finally, she feels she can have the Lord's undivided attention. Hannah is so moved, she doesn't notice anything around her. Her soul is wide open, and in her anguish, she begins to pour it out. She has but one request, one prayer, as old as her marriage itself. Her soul is weeping in silence, her lips are barely moving, not uttering any words, and an ember of hope begins to flicker within her heart.

The whole time she has been there, the priest has been watching, to him she appeared to be drunk, and like a bucket of cold water, Eli's anger pours over her kindled spirit.

Now what? How can it be that a servant of God, with years of ministry experience, could be so undiscerning about people? He should have shown at least some compassion. But no.

"Get out of the temple," he yells. "Drunken women everywhere, get out, go sober up!"

I can just imagine after getting this kind of "expert spiritual advice," anyone's desire to pray would have permanently vanished, not to mention that all respect for this sort of priesthood would have been lost as well.

Facing false accusations is difficult.

If only this man were more spiritually mature, he would surely understand everything. There was no need to come here. Talking to him now no longer makes any sense. How long can this go on? Maybe it's true, maybe I am cursed—everywhere I turn, there's a wall of conflict and misunderstanding. This is not fair! Why is this happening? Why me?

All these oppressive, imposing thoughts begin to fill her head, but Hannah dismisses them all, shrugging off the condemnation at her side, she guards her heart against resentment and "righteous" indignation. Years of pain and humiliation have not hardened her heart; instead, she has been deeply humbled by her suffering. "Not so, my lord," Hannah replied, "I am a woman who is deeply troubled. I have not been drinking wine or beer; I was pouring out my soul to the Lord. Do not take your servant for a wicked woman; I have been praying here out of my great anguish and grief" (1 Samuel 1:15–16).

> Years of pain and humiliation have not hardened her heart; instead, she has been deeply humbled by her suffering.

Eli, by now a very old man, the judge of Israel, looks deep into the eyes of this young woman. There is something painfully familiar in her eyes; the streaks of tears on her face and the depth of wrinkles on his own bear the evidence of their common suffering. She suffers because she is childless; he suffers because of his own children. Suddenly in this moment, in this sanctuary, both of them receive the answer to their anguished prayers, an answer that will become their greatest blessing.

Perhaps at this moment God revealed to Eli that there would be a new priestly judge in Israel who would anoint an unlikely shepherd, David, who would in turn become a great king of Israel.

"Go in peace, Hannah, and may the God of Israel grant you what you have asked of Him" (v. 17).

The silent anguish of her soul had reached the heavens. But no, she was not demanding justice, rather she was begging for mercy. Her heart passed the test of humility in the midst of her suffering. And the Lord gives grace to the humble. Those who seek Him receive mercy. Surprisingly, sometimes an answer arrives packaged as newborn sons. That day Hannah believed the priest one hundred percent! She knew her answer is on his way, so she stopped crying and began to rejoice right then, not after a month, not when she saw two pink lines on her pregnancy test, but she accepted her promise immediately.

> The Lord gives grace to the humble. Those who seek Him receive mercy.

Late night dinner, the food has gotten cold and the child in the arms of Elkanah had fallen asleep. Hardly anyone has noticed Hannah's temporary disappearance, but everyone notices her long-forgotten laughter and sudden change in her mood; they probably blamed it on the wine or other strong drink. But no, "The joy in the Lord is my strength" (Nehemiah 8:10), Hannah hums, gently taking Peninnah's sleeping child from her husband's arms and putting him to bed. And as she carries him, she cannot help but smile, imagining that soon she should be holding her own son in her arms.

Hannah named her firstborn son Samuel, which means "the Lord has heard" or "hearer of God." In his case, both meanings of his name turned out to be true, for both his mother and her son—God heard the mother and gave her a son who would become a man who heard from God. Then came time for Hannah to fulfill her own promise.

She brings her son to Eli. "I am the woman who stood here beside you praying to the Lord. I prayed for this child, and the Lord has granted me what I asked of Him" (1 Samuel 8:26–27).

Just a few years later, she stood in the Sanctuary of Shiloh again. But on that day, in place of her anguish, a song came bursting out from her heart, an anthem of praise, her personal revelation about the Lord—no, not the stuff you read in someone's book, but her own lived-out experience. She sang about the Lord to Whom she returned her boy, the Lord God Who had heard her, Who is holy, her stronghold, all-knowing and life-giving God. To Him she gave her long-awaited son. Yes, she then went home, but she came back every year to take care of Samuel and three other sons and two daughters, the children she birthed to her beloved husband.

HANNAH 1,000 YEARS AFTER

The same Bible that tells us about Hannah in the Old Testament tells about another Hannah on the pages of the New Testament. Although your Bible translation probably refers to her as Anna, the Latin form of her name, her name in Hebrew was the same: Hannah.

At first glance, the lives of these two women, separated by a thousand years, have nothing in common. What must a person do to be noticed or even mentioned on the pages of Scripture? How extraordinarily outstanding must their life be? The life of Hannah the Prophetess, whose whole life story fits into a few New Testament sentences, was seemingly unremarkable; nothing significant can be said about her, neither by us the readers nor by her peers. In all honesty, it can even be described as a tragic story.

> What must a person do to be noticed or even mentioned on the pages of Scripture? How extraordinarily outstanding must their life be?

Throughout history, in every culture, most girls dream about love, a happy marriage, and children, then grandchildren and a happy retirement surrounded by their loved ones. Back in those days in Middle Eastern culture, a girl would leave her parents very young as she joined her husband's household. In case of parental death, the orphaned children would inherit their father's estate, but after the death of her husband, his widow had no rights to his property. In this case, she had very few options: she could either return to her father's house or get married again. In times before feminism, financial independence and self-sufficiency did not apply to women; therefore, women could not support themselves. Widows automatically fell into the needy category; many would become homeless and downcast. For this reason the apostles gave specific instructions about widows and their ministry in the church. We can read about the kind of care and attention given to the widows and orphans in the New Testament.

Hannah's marital bliss ended tragically with the death of her husband. Her carefree childhood and seven years of happy marriage were gone as, suddenly, she became a young widow—a childless single woman. We will never know if she had any hope for remarriage nor if she could go back to her father's house. This will remain a mystery. We only know that Hannah chose to give her life to service in the Temple. She was probably about twenty-five when she first became a widow. When she finally met Jesus, the newborn baby brought to the Temple, she was eighty-four years old. Over fifty years of ministry, over half a century of worship, fasting, and prayers, day and night she poured her love on God and His people.

When did Hannah discover that God had given her the gift of prophecy? Who was it that first noticed and validated this gift in her? What was she doing in the Temple for all these years? It is written in the gospel that she "spoke of Him" to all who were awaiting redemption.

Two Witnesses

Scripture tells us that every truth is validated by the testimony of two witnesses. After Jesus was born, on the eighth day, Joseph and Mary brought him into the Temple, where they offered a sacrifice according to the Law of Moses and gave the baby a name. That is where Simeon and Hannah met their Messiah, and being moved by the Holy Spirit, they confirmed His arrival.

What are the chances that an obscure provincial couple from the small village of Nazareth would have a chance to meet Hannah in that crowded Temple? What are the chances that she would recognize them, and moreover, that she would see the Messiah in their helpless little newborn? Every Jew had been awaiting the coming of the Messiah; they all believed the Redeemer would come like a strong military leader and would free them from the oppression of the hated Roman Empire.

But prophets can see people and situations the way God sees them; they proclaim a message from the Lord. Eight days after the first Christmas, on an ordinary day, among the bleating of the sheep and the cooing of caged pigeons, among the noise of merchants, pilgrims, priests, the Pharisees, and Sadducees, there in the middle of it all stood an old woman with a baby in her arms.

Joseph and Mary have become accustomed to supernatural events surrounding them this past year. They stand in awe and reverence, silently watching this mysterious encounter. For Hannah, this was not her first time meeting the

> This was not her first time meeting the Lord—they know each other very well—but she has waited her whole life for this particular meeting.

Lord—they know each other very well—but she has waited her whole life for this particular meeting. She has been hastening the coming of the Messiah into our world with her intercessions and prayers.

Hannah, the eighty-four-year-old woman, and Jesus, an eight-day-old infant. Her mission has ended; His mission is just beginning.

Both Hannahs had prayed different prayers in different centuries, but in truth, they were very much the same. One begged for a son who became a judge and a prophet. The other prayed for the coming of the Son of God into this world, the promised Messiah. Both Hannahs prayed in the sanctuary. The answer to both of their prayers was a son—the Son of God Who would become a blessing to so many.

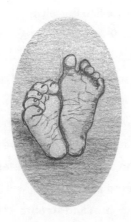

• LIFE LESSONS •

ABOUT GOD. God holds our destiny in His hand. **"Lord, you alone are my portion and my cup; you make my lot secure" (Psalm 15:5).** A fate of failure can becomes a great destiny when we rise above ourselves and begin to look at things with the heavenly perspective.

ABOUT US. Our reaction to false accusations and misunderstandings is a kind of litmus test for our soul. Given a bit of pressure, that which fills our heart begins to come right out. **"A gentle answer turns away wrath, but a harsh word stirs up anger" (Proverbs 15:1).**

ABOUT LIFE. Life is not fair. Disgraceful women become pregnant and kill their babies. Virtuous women are trying to get pregnant and can't. Often, we find ourselves in circumstances that are not of our own choosing, but how we react to them is always up to us. In times of difficulty, when we can't make sense of our predicament and there are many unanswered questions, some people succumb to blaming others for their pain. This puts them on a path to victimhood. Unable to find peace, they spend all their energy on self-pity and bitterness. Yet, we have a promise: **"And the God of all grace, who called you to his eternal glory in Christ, after you have suffered a little while, will himself restore you and make you strong, firm and steadfast" (1 Peter 5:10).**

ABOUT HUMILITY. As our hearts become soft, and the divine seeds of hope and faith are placed within us, then our tears of suffering are like life-giving water to them. Give it some time and those seeds will sprout. The Lord will lead you from surrounding festivities, from your kitchen table, into His temple. There will be a season when everyone around you will have fun and joy, but you will be weeping and praying. But, **"Those who sow with tears will reap with songs of joy. Those who go out weeping, carrying seed to sow, will return with songs of joy, carrying sheaves with them" (Psalm 126:5–6).**

ABOUT LOYALTY. Loyal devotion keeps its promises. It's funny how fervently people promise things out of desperation. We will promise anything—we will promise you the moon. But then, as things settle and everything works out, we think, Oh no, did I promise a bit too much? Nevertheless, be a keeper of your word, and you shall reap its blessing. **"It is better not to make a vow than to make one and not fulfill it" (Ecclesiastes 5:4).**

JULIA.
A SONG OF A DAUGHTER

A black Toyota Highlander zips along the highway, a smooth ebony-like ribbon divided by a double yellow line. Like a thin, barely noticeable thread of hair, the highway twists and turns on the background of towering evergreen forests amid the picturesque mountains of Oregon. Every new turn reveals new breathtaking landscapes, and I grumble at the fact that there aren't enough viewpoints for us to stop along the way. At times, I ask my husband to stop right on the side of the highway; I don't want to miss any of this beauty speeding past my window. He stops. I get out of the car for a few minutes and soak it all in.

I've been hoping to visit this beautiful place for a few years now—located right in the heart of Oregon—Crater Lake. You can only get there by car and only in the summer. The mountain passes around the lake become inaccessible due to the snow, and from autumn to spring the road is closed. We wait for our children to grow up a bit so that this five-hour trip will be fun for everyone. And this summer, instead of going on vacation to someplace exotic, we have planned a cross-country, low-budget car trip exploring Pacific Northwest Oregon and California coasts. Our first stop is Crater Lake.

We live right on the border of Washington and Oregon, so we travel by way of Interstate 5. We start heading south, then continue 50 miles east to the interior of the continent. As we travel, there are lakes, waterfalls, majestic trees all around. We read the road signs and from time to time take spontaneous turns to unexplored waterfalls. Struck by this majestic scenery, we discover that we were completely unaware of the existence of such incredibly beautiful places. Like most immigrants in their new country, in the beginning we had to work very hard, and because of that, we did not travel much.

As we journey on, the climate starts changing, the temperature rises, the trees become shorter and shorter, the green grass is replaced by a shriveled yellow landscape, and all around the ground looks scorched, revealing evidence of ancient lava flows. We are approaching the crater of a magnificent volcano like a beautiful bowl filled to the brim with the reflection of endless blue.

Our car has a CD player, but we hardly ever use it. Nowadays, most of our music comes from downloads on our phones. The kids take turns connecting their phones to the car speakers and playing their favorite songs. Sometimes we listen to the music on the radio. But the last couple of years, one particular disc has been playing in our CD player, a disc with very unusual music. We listen to it when we are driving outside the city through the beautiful countryside, on long trips, just like this one. The disc is only forty-five minutes long, but the music is so profound. It is quite different from our usual playlist, not at all like the typical three verses and a chorus. This disc was recorded by the group Dunamis, and the artists are Julia and Alex, our dear friends.

* * *

We met Julia at a friend's house, where we learned that she teaches music. Our daughter Katerina is an aspiring singer, and in a few months Julia began giving lessons to our children. Unfortunately I did not always manage to come with them, but the children instantly fell in love with their new teacher. My husband and I admired her professionalism and her clear beautiful voice.

A few years went by. Julia went on maternity leave and returned back to classes after the birth to her daughter. Our children sang, played, sometimes they even participated in the children's program at church, and they were always so happy to see Julia. How could they love a teacher who gave them homework to stretch their abilities? Could it be that the chil-

> How could they love a teacher who gave them homework to stretch their abilities? Could it be that all children simply love those who truly love them?

dren felt love not so much toward a teacher, a coach, or a pastor, but rather, all children simply love those who truly love them?

What a fascinating person our Julia is. She is very young yet truly mature; talented but not proud; strong but not defiant; humble yet uncrushed. She is open hearted but never oversteps boundaries. She is always full of joy, positivity, and inspiration. I always think of her as my equal, simply forgetting how young she really is. Honestly, if I had given birth at sixteen, she could have been my daughter. Everyone is surprised when they find out how old she actually is, and she herself feels a bit awkward, finding out how old people think she is. As I think about her, carefully studying her beautiful, young face, I realize there's something about her that is not skin deep; it is something different. It's maturity.

I do not know anything about her family's background. What was her childhood like? Who are her parents? How did they manage to raise such a wonderful, kind, and hardworking girl? How were they able to instill in her the value of love and respect for other people? Eventually, after dozens, or more like hundreds, of lessons and visits to our home, after we had drunk multiple cups of tea together, the door to her past began to slowly open. And as I looked through it, I started to see something absolutely unexpected.

Somewhere, in the very distant village of Russia's Far East, stands a small off-the-grid house without running water. It is a home for a little girl, her younger brother, their grandmother, and their mother, who is an alcoholic. Dad is nowhere to be found. Of course, there was a man who gave life to these children, but no one knows where he is.

A five year old girl is playing with her friends on the dirt road. She returns home to find her little three-year-old brother sitting in the middle of a mud puddle in the yard crying. He shivers from the cold or from hunger or in fear of being alone. She takes him inside the house, she washes him and changes his clothes, and then they sit and wait for their grandmother to return. She is the one who takes care of them. They wait together late into the night.

It was over twenty years ago, but Julia remembers it as if she is still there, standing in the middle of her street, seeing someone helping to drag her intoxicated mother, who can barely stand on her own feet, home. Julia has mixed feelings about her mother; she feels shame on account of her friends, but at the same time, she feels strong love for her mom. *After she sleeps it off and washes up, everything will be fine again. She is my mom, my dearest, she is all I have. My one and only.*

The girl is eight years old. Nobody pays much attention to her. But she keeps a diary where she writes down her dreams and desires. If I could be there, I would tell her, *Make a wish, baby girl. Make a wish and write it down.*

First, I want for my mom to stop drinking. Second, I want a horse.

Keep writing, little Julia—hopes and dreams do come true. And even though you do not know Him yet, He is already there with you, right in your room. Be patient dear; none of this is pointless;

your dreams will come to pass in time. One day your Momma will stop drinking, she will become beautiful and healthy again, and you will be able to talk to her about everything in the world.

Maybe you won't get a real horse with a long silky tail, but one day your beautiful Honda will have more than a dozen horse-powers! You still have a few testing years of character forging left, but they won't break your spirit. Your spirit will only become stronger.

They say we don't choose our own family. Julia was sitting in my dining room, drinking coffee, when she said, "If I were to choose, I would have chosen her, only her—my mom. I would leave absolutely everything as it was. Even those vicious teen-girl fights, when you know that you don't have a dad or an older brother to protect you. When all you have is guts. That, and strong arms, the hands of a future pianist, that can grab hold of someone's hair and fight back, when push comes to shove."

After the fight, she tries to find her broken glasses, smashed on the ground, looking for them through tears while expletives and curses still ring in her ears. When she finally makes it home, instead of love, sympathy, and understanding, she finds her house trashed, strange people sleeping everywhere after a recent drinking party they must have shared with her mother—the kind of party that hollows out the soul and leaves one in godless misery.

Is there no one I can confide in? Is there anyone I can share hopes and dreams with? Is anyone at all interested in what's important?

And so, this child poured her soul out onto the pages of her diary (she still has that diary, by the way), but she should not have trusted it to keep her secrets. Each line was carefully read by Someone who cared about every detail, Someone Who could provide much more than her desires or dreams.

She writes:

I love music. I feel that there is something magical in music, something extraordinary...

Furthermore, Julia can sing.

Well, at this time, let us just say she wants to sing, rather than she *can* sing.

Hallelujah, she is chosen to sing in the school choir. Even though usually all the best spots are reserved for the "best" kids. Julia isn't one of them; her mom never comes to any parent conferences, she never brings her teachers gifts, and she never even asked her teachers to pay attention to her talented little girl. When her classmates complain how their parents make them go to music school and that they *must* study, how terrible it is for them, Julia cannot believe her ears. Music school is not free. At this age, Julia is old enough not to ask stupid questions at home. She knows the answer will be the same as to all the other questions: We don't have any money.

Still, the ways of the Lord are deeply mysterious, aren't they? Her choir teacher enters Julia into a vocal competition, an event held at the House of Culture, and she gives her a solo part to sing. Seated on that jury is the Director of the Music School along with a few local business owners. One of them notices the girl wearing glasses who won the Grand Prize. He cannot get this child out of his mind. The Director asks her teacher, "Why is this girl not enrolled in the music school?" When he is given the reason, the business owner decides to become her sponsor. At last, Julia is a music school student studying piano. Amazingly, she learns how to play an instrument that she doesn't even have at home.

Yet the Father—the One Who gifted her with her talent and an ability to learn—more than anything, is waiting for her to meet with Him. This needy teenage girl from a dysfunctional family, cross-eyed with crooked teeth yet with the biggest of hearts, comes to church one day and finally meets Him, beginning the process of her own heart's transformation.

She is getting to know love, the kind that will become her father, her mother, and her older brother.

When she encountered the Father, she fell in love with Him, and she received everything that she ever needed—the love of God.

Not only did Julia find her Savior, but in church she found a family—brothers and sisters. There, she also met a tall and handsome young man, Alex. Alex played the guitar, and together they served in worship and music ministry and both loved the Lord with all their hearts. A few years later they married, and the young couple began to build their own family on a strong foundation: God

> When she encountered the Father, she fell in love with Him, and she received everything that she ever needed—the love of God.

and their sense of oneness. Despite malicious voices reminding them that children are doomed to repeat their parents' miserable fate, Julia and Alex firmly and fervently believed that all who trust in God shall be renewed and blessed by Him—both the husband and the wife, as well as their future children. They both dedicated their life to God, knowing that their life is not a repetition of someone else's fate, but a blessed and uncommon future—a divine destiny.

> They both dedicated their life to God, knowing that their life is not a repetition of someone else's fate, but a blessed and uncommon future—a divine destiny.

Julia studied at the Khabarovsk Regional College of Art. A few years later she became a trained classical opera performing artist. The stage of the Khabarovsk Philharmonic Theater, where she was the leading opera soloist, was only the beginning. When Alex and Julia moved to the United States, they began attending a local church and leading worship. They also write music and compose songs. Leading people in worship is what they do best, their calling; their hearts are overjoyed as they lead worshipers into the presence of the Father to adore and praise Him. The Lord blessed them with a beautiful baby girl, Nicole, and a completely new world opened up for them—motherhood and fatherhood. Soon after, another door opened, and our opera singer, Julia, took part in a concert with an orchestra at the Hampton Opera Center in Portland, Oregon.

Julia's heavenly Father has truly blessed her.

As an adoption process gets finalized, after a court issues the final approval, the child's last name is officially changed to that of the new parents, and the child becomes their own son or daughter. In the case of an abandoned baby, this process is easier—the child grows with the adoptive parents. The first words, *Mama* and *Dada*, as well as the first love and hugs all belong to those who adopted.

Infants may never even know that they are not their parents' biological children. However, in the case of older children, when they are adopted, the court decision alone does not actually make them feel that they are sons or daughters to their new parents in the true sense. That sense of truly belonging depends upon a process of getting to know each other, trusting, accepting, and opening hearts and souls to one another. The Bible tells us that God, through Jesus, has adopted us all; hence, each one of us is going through their own journey of getting to know our heavenly Father.

Years later, after she was already married, Julia had this unique encounter with her heavenly Daddy, the One Who had adopted and accepted her—to Whom she wrote her whole diary, filled with her letters of prayer. She was truly happy, but still, that helpless little girl continued to live on inside her, and the wounds of her past would resurface and bleed again from time to time. She desperately needed a spiritual healing, a transplantation of the heart so that her memories of the past would no longer ache and bleed, so that she could stop shrinking from depression and self-pity.

During that personal encounter, amid the silence and solitude, it was as if her heavenly Father transferred her back to that old house in the Far East. There she saw a frightened, little girl in a dress that was dirty and torn. For some reason, the little girl was kept in a dungeon—the cold and dark part of the house where no one lived or ever entered. It was dark, damp, and lonely—just as it would be in the heart of someone who was not given enough love and attention.

But even there, she was never alone; Dad was there with her. He opened the door, took that little girl by the hand, and led her out of there never to return. And she was standing next to Him in a brightly warm room, wearing a beautiful new dress, warmed by something larger than the sun itself—by His love.

This was little Julia's personal exodus to her own promised land—God had prepared a destiny for her, centuries before she was even born. She will forget her own Egypt, but she will never stop thanking Him Who brought her out and will never stop singing about Him and for Him alone.

* * *

So, back to the disc that was playing in our car. These were not your usual songs in the usual sense. They were not just words put to music; these were the songs from deep within one's soul.

> Admiring the mountains, the evergreen forests, and lakes, it seems this music must have been written right here in this place—it is a perfect match for this scenery.

They are flows of sound, groans, and cries, extraordinarily beautiful harmonies that are so deep that they reach to the furthest corners of my soul. There aren't adequate words to describe them, neither in beautiful English nor in the rich language of Tolstoy, Dostoevsky, and Pushkin to express what she is feeling. I am mesmerized. Admiring the mountains, the evergreen forests, and lakes outside my window, it seems this music must have been written right here in this place—it is a perfect match for this scenery. A song to the Creator, Who created our ancient universe, the One Who continues to create new hearts and new destinies even today.

Do you know what a miracle is? The authentic supernatural, beyond the laws of physics and logic? A miracle is when the blind receive their sight, when new organs and tissue begin to appear, when the limbs of a crippled person suddenly grow in front of your eyes. Who among us does not want to witness a miracle; wouldn't we love to experience it?

This is my understanding of miracles. These days, after centuries of technological and medical advances, things that in previous centuries required miracles are made possible for us because of the scientific progress. To some extent, man has made the impossible possible today. But not everything. And not for everyone. There are still things that only God can heal, just as two centuries ago. Humankind has flown into space, has descended to the bottom of the deepest oceans, and is capable of complicated procedures like a heart transplant, but humanity still can't manage to make

> To some extent, man has made the impossible possible today. But not everything. And not for everyone. There are still things that only God can heal, just as two centuries ago.

one abused little girl raised in the dungeon happy. There are no tools or technologies available that can transform her heart and mind. Her happiness does not depend on her wearing new dresses or straightening crooked teeth, and training her voice—not even her success and her diploma—makes no difference. What finally turned that little girl around and gave her true happiness is love. Love triumphantly led her by the hand out of that dungeon. Love placed her on top of the mountain where I was now standing in awe and admiration of the vastness of the expanse. And Love said, *My dear daughter, this is all yours. I created this whole world for you.*

Have I ever seen a miracle? Yes, many times. In fact, I am witnessing a miracle when I talk to Julia. The story of her past would have been the perfect narrative for perpetuating a victimhood portfolio, endlessly retelling her miserable life story to live off the sympathy and compassion drawn from others. But no! Instead, Julia appears to be a very well educated and talented young lady from an intelligent family—because this is the reality of her life now. And yes, somewhere in Russia's Far Eastern town, there still lives a beautiful, slender woman with a very stylish haircut—Julia's mom. You would never believe who she was fifteen or twenty years ago. Julia constantly talks to her via Skype, and now she and her mom have a trusting, loving, and meaningful relationship. But her Daddy is much closer than the Far East, very, very close. Of course, she now has the best parents possible!

Again and again, I hear, "Your name is above every other name." It seems that she can endlessly sing just this one phrase, Your name. Her heart, renewed and restored, is now strong and overflowing with love, and it pours out in inexpressible words and sounds. And when she manages to envelop her songs within human language, poems like these are born:

> I cannot be silent
> About what You have done.
> I cannot be silent
> About Who You are to me.

Please, don't be silent, Julia, sing out this glorious song, the song of a grateful daughter. Julia, you and Crater Lake are so much alike; you are extraordinary, like a majestic bowl filled to the brim with the reflections of heaven.

• LIFE LESSONS •

ABOUT GOD. God is our Father. He can and wants to become our own Father and Mother—our family. I think most of us Christians know this, and almost every one of us turns to Him with the words Our Father Who art in heaven in our daily prayers.

Jesus came to introduce us to the Father to show us what the Father is like. Everyone at some point in life receives this revelation about the Fatherhood of God, and that encounter changes us forever. Because this revelation is not head knowledge of pure facts, it takes place within our hearts and changes our souls forever, by making us believers, which equals people who are saved from hell, making us God's sons and daughters. **"And do not call anyone on earth 'father,' for you have one Father, and he is in heaven"** (Matthew 23:9).

ABOUT US. A mature and well-rounded person is someone who values his own spiritual health. For this very reason, God sent his Son, to revive our spirits and to restore us back to the Father. Jesus Christ not only suffered and died for us, redeeming us from our sins, but moreover, He has restored us back to the fullness of life with God, opening the way for our own spiritual and physical healing.

"May God himself, the God of peace, sanctify you through and through. May your whole spirit, soul and body be kept blameless at the coming of our Lord Jesus Christ" (1 Thessalonians 5:23).

ABOUT LIFE. It is impossible to attain fulfillment unless we learn how to forgive. Unforgiveness is like an amputation of our spiritual wings. By forgiving others, we ourselves become Christlike—for the Lord Himself forgives us constantly, endlessly, and unconditionally. Sometimes we forget that by forgiving others, we do ourselves a favor; we become free from the poison of bitterness and resentment eating away at our hearts from within, poisoning our whole life. Forgiveness is not denial of the offense. It is not an absolution of one's guilt or responsibility for the consequences of their actions. Neither is it an obligation to trust the offender again and to maintain a relationship. Realizing this can make forgiveness easier. To forgive is to let go of the guilt as well as the offense. We will never be able to rise if we are pressed to the ground by the burden of offense and unforgiveness. Moreover, we are instructed to forgive—it is God's commandment. **"And when you stand praying, if you hold anything against anyone, forgive them, so that your Father in heaven may forgive you your sins"(Mark 11:25).**

ABOUT TALENTS. God has given each of us gifts, abilities, and talents, He also gave us the desire to grow and develop in them. Yet the responsibility to discover and develop our divine gifts and how and in what way we shall use them is entirely up to us. In the parable of the talents, Jesus says that God gave everyone a different amount of talents, but no one was deprived; everyone got something without exception.

"There are different kinds of gifts, but the same Spirit distributes them. There are different kinds of service, but the same Lord. There are different kinds of working, but in all of them and in everyone it is the same God at work." (1 Corinthians 12:4–6)

ABOUT MUSIC. Musical and vocal abilities are not for the exclusive use of a few gifted people, even though it can be their career or hobby. The Bible emphasizes the importance of expressing our devotion to God through music, dedicating a whole book to it, a collection of psalms, which are prayers expressed in song. When we sing psalms, we do two things. First, we give praise and thanksgiving to God, singing about Him and to Him alone. Second, we uplift one another. **"Be filled with the Spirit, speaking to one another with psalms, hymns, and songs from the Spirit. Sing and make music from your heart to the Lord"** (Ephesians 5:18–19).

One time I was observing, or rather, I was listening to the process of recording the audio recording for our worship group in a studio setting. There in the recording room, the group sounded harmoniously beautiful: Sopranos, altos, tenors, keys, guitars, drums all sounded as one whole, in unison. But then, in the studio, each instrument and each vocal could be listened to separately, because each was recorded on a separate track. I remember, how clearly I heard in my heart: This is how God hears each one of us—as if everything else and everyone else becomes silent, and all He listens to is my voice, my prayer, and my song alone. And no matter what type of vocal ability I possess, He relishes the purity and sincerity of my heart's feelings. Therefore, do not be a spectator or an audience, but become part of the corporate worship, because your Father is standing right there, beside you, and His ear is inclined to your heart!

EVE.
LIFE AFTER DEATH

Living in America and not driving a car is possible only in big cities that have a system of well-developed public transportation, some place like New York or Los Angeles. I was 18 when I got my driver's license back in Russia, but I only drove a couple of times. The reason for my misfortune is that I happened to scratch someone else's car with the broken headlight of my dad's new Moskvich-2141 as I was backing out of a parking lot; I scratched the side of my dad's car as well. Dad repaired both cars without a single word of resentment, but I put my driving license on the shelf until another time. Ten years later, my husband and I were living in America, and getting around our city without a car was absolutely impossible. Vasily brought me the study guide for the driving test, and a few days later I took the exam. I easily passed the written part of the test, they snapped a picture of me, grinning from ear to ear. Then they handed me my driving permit and scheduled another date for my driving test.

I'm not sure whether it was my overconfidence or the presence of my Russian driver's license on the shelf or maybe it was my sweet encouraging husband overpraising me while he was sitting in the passenger seat, but I failed my first driving test. I remember my first reaction: I was ashamed, and I felt like I needed to find the reason for my failure, so I had to talk about it with everyone I know. *The instructor was a woman, and she didn't like me, so she failed me. Of course I can drive a car. My husband is confidently sitting right next to me, my baby daughter is in the back in her car seat; I really am capable of driving a vehicle.*

But the second time, the instructor was a man, and I again failed the exam. And again, I was looking for someone to blame, a good excuse. *It must be because there are so many immigrants in Portland, and not everybody likes that, so the instructors are biased; that is the reason he failed me. Why would anyone deliberately tell me to turn right onto oncoming one-way traffic?*

Something is clearly wrong here; I don't even want to reschedule my test anymore. How many months can I drive with just my driving permit? No, eventually I will still have to pass this test. I need to do something about this. I asked my husband, "Why do you think I failed?"

He smiled back and shrugged his shoulders, clearly hinting that I should take a closer look at myself. So, I went to the "Higher Authority" and asked there, finally realizing that there's no need to look for excuses. The instructors were doing their job, and most likely I was just too confident and not paying enough attention. Hence I repented. The good Lord forgave me, and I declared again and again, that everything, absolutely everything in my life is from God and with His help—always! Finally on my third try, together with Jesus, I got my driver's license, and since then we always drive together.

> I repented. The good Lord forgave me, and I declared again and again, that everything, absolutely everything in my life is from God and with His help—always!

Both before and after this episode, there were many failed tests in my life. Like most of us, my first reaction to failure, or should I say getting an F, is a ready list of good excuses and even valid justifications. We all can finger point, shifting the blame to everyone and everything else: the president, the state, the laws, the weather, the family, my friends, misfortune, and even bad luck. The habit of shifting the blame is as old as humanity—and it seems that it has been passed down to us from the very first humans, Adam and Eve. But in retrospect, the story of the first people can also teach us how to live with the consequences of our choices and mistakes. And what it takes to keep on living, overcoming all obstacles and continuing to thrive.

Life After the Biggest Failure in the History of Newly-Created Humanity

Everyone dreams of living in paradise, meaning living in peace and prosperity devoid of all suffering. People are willing to work for months, even years, to be able to escape the daily grind for that long-awaited vacation for a few weeks—a tropical version of paradise. The sun, the sand, the beach, and the hammock between two palm trees—a picture of life in paradise! But what if you live like this every day, twenty-four seven? What would that be like? An "all inclusive" lifestyle—no work, no disease, no stress of any kind? We, of course, might think that if it were up to us, we would not jeopardize this kind of life for anything. Many of us think that we would have been smarter than our ancestors, since Adam and Eve proved to be incapable of overcoming their temptation and as a result lost their paradise, not only for themselves but for humanity as a whole.

The story of Eve's life is the story of a woman who probably suffered the deepest of contradictions, anguish, and turmoil. She was the first participant in this tragedy that separated men from God, and she was also the first to continue the human race. Death came through her, but life came through her as well. This is the story of the very first woman, the very first wife, and the very first mother.

"In the beginning."

How did it all begin?

Was this story a myth, a metaphor, or was it a narrative of real events that took place exactly as it is written in the first chapters of the first book of the Bible, Genesis? In six days, God created our planet, the sun, the moon, and the stars, the continents and the oceans with plants and animals. And in the end, He created mankind. This is the ultimate mystery of our universe, and it shall remain a mystery. For centuries the greatest minds have pondered the origin of it all, thousands of volumes of theological works have been written, but there are still thousands of questions that remain unanswered. It shall forever be a mystery.

Incomprehensible is the love of our Creator, Who formed this magnificent universe, hanging our earth on nothing amid the vastness of surrounding galaxies, and then, on this tiniest of specks, in the very center of our planet, He planted a beautiful garden. He did all this in preparation—like decorating the scene, in anticipation of the appearance of history's' main character, mankind, the crown jewel of God's finished work of art and the culmination of His creative endeavor.

> **So God created mankind in his own image, in the image of God he created him; male and female he created them. God blessed them and**

said to them, "Be fruitful and increase in number; fill the earth and subdue it." (Genesis 1:27–28)

Eve—what was she like? She must have been the picture of perfection, absolutely everything that God made had the stamp on perfection on it. "It was very good" (Genesis 1:31). Her life with Adam must have been perfect. After all, they were sinless, free of any accusation, offense, insult, envy, and unforgiveness. Her perception of her husband was that of a perfect man, and she must have been profoundly happy. Unfortunately she must have got a bit bored with her picture-perfect life, and she probably yearned for something exciting and unknown.

Or maybe she simply felt left out by her own husband, or maybe even by God Himself. Eve's inquisitive mind thirsted after new experiences. She was craving knowledge; after all, they were not preprogrammed robots. God created them as free beings, and to her the forbidden nature of the tree in the midst of the garden seemed completely useless and unnecessary. The serpent himself did not appear to be a malevolent creature that would bring temptation, sin, and damnation to humanity. Her naive mind, free of our accumulated knowledge and experience, could not perceive any immediate danger—this was simply an opportunity for an interesting conversation. She faced a manipulation she had never encountered as

> She faced a manipulation she had never encountered as her companion, the serpent, gently nudged her to question everything with honesty and to simply speak her own mind.

her companion, the serpent, gently nudged her to question everything with honesty and to simply speak her own mind.

You never know until you try, they say. How can you know if something is genuinely true? "Hath God said?" (Genesis 3:1 KJV). There are only two options: The first is to know the One Who is speaking and to trust His honesty, believing in the authenticity of His words; and the second is to dismiss His words and learn from one's own experience. If there were no options, then there would be no free will, because freedom means choice. This was the whole reason behind that ill-fated tree planted right in the middle of that beautiful garden, a tree of forbidden fruit—anyone who eats from it "shall surely die" (Genesis 2:17 KJV). As the coils of the cunning serpent wrapped around the branches of the tree, he softly spoke hypnotizing words, invoking lies and appealing to Eve's vanity. Whispering under the rustle of the leaves, he was stroking her ego and arousing her sudden eagerness to become godlike.

Only one move, and she was holding the fruit in her hand. Then tragedy struck—as soon as she put it to her lips and tasted its rich flesh, the earth experienced a cosmic shift. An invisible explosion of atomic proportions produced a shockwave that would permanently infect every human living on our planet. In that moment corruption seeped into every cell of her body with lightning speed. Together with the juicy pulp of the fruit, it permeated her body and then that of Adam as well. Death crept in slowly and began to lay waste to their perfectly created bodies and souls.

This is how sin entered the world—the greatest tragedy in the history of mankind. Eve never could have known the weight of her actions as she was reaching for the fruit. She couldn't have grasped how long the consequences of her venture would continue to echo throughout all humanity. While sharing that half-bitten fruit with her husband, she still couldn't know that she would have to experience "shall surely die" in full color, not only through their spiritual depravity, not only through her own death, but what was to be more devastating was to experience death as it takes someone you love, and you are completely powerless to change anything.

Their paradise vacation ended abruptly. Suddenly from somewhere within, mysterious voices of conscience began to shout thoughts of self-pity and regret. Moments before, they had been perfect and beautiful. Now, suddenly, they were naked and ashamed. The weight of guilt and shame crushed them like a massive concrete slab. Seeing each other's nakedness, they no longer felt perfectly innocent.

> Suddenly from somewhere within, mysterious voices of conscience began to shout thoughts of self-pity and regret. Moments before, they had been perfect and beautiful. Now, suddenly, they were naked and ashamed.

It seems that by taking advantage of their freedom of choice, they forever lost their freedom, forfeiting their potential to truly be themselves, to walk freely without hiding. They lost their ability to freely stand in the presence of God and to commune with Him. But this was only the beginning of their depravity. Their loss was exponential and utterly catastrophic, so much so that their redemption would have to come at an enormous cost, and there was only one possibility that could overcome their depravity, the cost of the most valued possession in the whole universe. It would cost God the life of His own Son.

But that was still to come. For now they had to witness the death of animals, whose hides became their clothes, and like that, they left the Garden of Eden forever. How could this be? Just the day before, God was so close, He interacted with them with so much love, but today an angel with a sword of flame was standing at the gate, and they are forbidden His presence. What now? This garden was created just for them, and cultivating it was their life's mission!

Suddenly their whole vocabulary had been drastically amended: words like *illness, death, thorns, thistles, curse,* and *sweat* come into use. What did all this mean? They were used to quite the opposite—God would bring the animals to Adam, who would gave them names. And now they heard new and unknown words, the meaning of which Adam and Eve would have to learn by experience.

Outside of Paradise, life continued. They lived by the sweat of their brow, afflicted with sickness and disease. Eve gave birth to Cain and Abel. She became the first mother, and yes, she was the very first woman to experience giving birth, the first to experience the consequences of her own sin—"with painful labor you will give birth to children" (Genesis 3:16), yet at the same time, she was the first to experience the joy and happiness of motherhood as well.

I can imagine how Adam and Eve raised their boys, how they introduced them to our wonderful world, how they taught them the names of all the animals that Adam himself once named. I can just imagine how they told them stories about their former life in the Garden of Eden, how they taught them about God their Creator, about sin and its consequences and about their common enemy. Perhaps they recounted their conversations with God to them, telling their kids what they talked to Him about as they strolled along the garden paths together in the coolness of the evening, back in those beautiful days. Unfortunately their sons could never know that kind of life.

Many parents who have more than two kids sometimes wonder how they can be so different. We raise them the same way, teaching them the very same things. Perhaps they learn and listen to us a bit differently. And then by virtue of the truths and principles adopted by them, they end up living according to those different ways. It turns out that people worship God in different ways as well, even those who listen to the exact same stories about Him, much like these brothers, the sons of Adam and Eve. They both seemed to have knowledge about God, they both served Him, but each had his own motives for doing so. Not surpris-

> Many parents who have more than two kids sometimes wonder how they can be so different.

ingly, God would look on their sacrifices based on their inner motives and not on the superior quality of the offering itself.

"The Lord looked with favor on Abel and his offering, but on Cain and his offering he did not look with favor. So Cain was very angry, and his face was downcast" (Genesis 4:4–5). Most of us usually stop right here, and we think that the tragedy between two brothers was because of Cain's emotional reaction to God's rejection of his offering. But if we keep reading, we can see that when God rejected Cain's sacrifice, He did not stop there. He continued talking to him and immediately pointed at the reason for his rejection. In fact, with His profound questions, God was trying to teach Cain a valuable lesson—instead of focusing on his burnt offering, God was bringing attention to what was burning in Cain's heart. God shed light on his inner problem, and He implored Cain to "rule over sin" that was already "crouching at the door" of his heart (v. 7).

But Cain turned out to be the third person possessing uninhibited freedom of will. And he would use his God-given freedom of choice by completely disregarding his Creator's advice. Instead, he invited his younger brother to take a walk in the field. "While they were in the field, Cain attacked his brother Abel and killed him" (Genesis 4:8).

> Cain turned out to be the third person possessing uninhibited freedom of will. And he would use his God-given freedom of choice by completely disregarding his Creator's advice.

Abel is dead. What is death? Was there ever a need for a dictionary in the Garden of Eden? For newly created people, everything in their new world was new. How do we learn a new word if we are unfamiliar with the concept behind it? How are we to comprehend or to explain something that has never once happened before, not to you nor to anyone else ever? Eve sat on the ground, holding her blood-covered son in her arms, unable to wake him up from his cold deep sleep. He would never be awakened. It would take her some time, but Eve would know the meaning of death by tasting the pain and grief of her own loss.

Am I dreaming or am I awake? The Garden of Eden must have been only a beautiful dream, or maybe it's the other way around. Is what's happening now a horrible nightmare?

Now after death has shown its ugly face, how shall we live?

What for?

For whom?

One of her son's was dead and the other cast out and cursed by God. "And Cain went out from the Lord's presence and dwelt in the land of Nod, east of Eden" (Genesis 4:16). Once again Adam and Eve were all alone. Sometimes life is like a roller-coaster ride—one moment is picture perfect, the next we fall to the bottom of despair and grief. We can step from heaven to hell while still being on earth. But we must strive upward, remembering what God has commanded: "Be fruitful and multiply and replenish the earth and subdue it" (Genesis 1:28). You were created in His own image and His own likeness, which means you are endowed with the power to create and give life.

"Adam made love to his wife again, and she gave birth to a son and named him Seth, saying, 'God has granted me another child in place of Abel, since Cain killed him.'" (Genesis 4:25). So it is, in this one Bible verse, in one sentence, she named all three of her sons along with God the Creator who gives life and extends our legacy. She gave birth to her third boy and gave him the name that would determine his destiny—*Appointed*; he was appointed to continue the race and to be the carrier of God's divine seed of life.

I wonder how they chose names for their children. They must have had a remarkable experience doing just that with animals. By giving names to hundreds and thousands of animals, birds, and fish, Adam could easily have made a career in zoology today. But it is one thing to name something that already exists, something that is right in front of you, and it is something completely different to hear a word without seeing what it represents.

Looking back at the beginning, we should notice something remarkable that took place between the first couple after the fall and their expulsion from Paradise the Book of Genesis says: "Adam named his wife Eve, because she became the mother of all the living" (Genesis 3:20). Right after they were separated from God, after being kicked out from Paradise, after becoming spiritually deprived Adam did not blame his wife for the fact that she conspired

> Adam did not blame his wife ...He didn't call her dumb or stupid or pitiful or dreadful. He didn't condemn her as the sole cause of all his misery. He gave her a name full of positivity.

with the serpent and took it upon herself to eat of the forbidden fruit. He didn't call her dumb or stupid or pitiful or dreadful. He didn't condemn her as the sole cause of all his misery. He gave her a name full of positivity—Eve; that means *Life*!

Eve's name depicted her essence. She survived the death of one of her children, and living through the pain and suffering of death, she continued to give life. Of course, Adam could not come up with a better name for his wife, a name that would perfectly reflect her essence and her divine purpose. Seth also lived up to his name. He inherited faith in God and a longing to commune with Him. "Seth also had a son, and he called his name Enosh. At that time people began to call on the name of the Lord" (Genesis 4:26). The fellowship that had been interrupted by sin was beginning to be restored.

God's love for mankind never ceased, and He yearns to fellowship with us. Seth had heard His call within his heart, and he responded to it wholeheartedly. This was the very first step of restoration of the paradise lost by mankind. Because what made the Garden of Eden into Paradise was unhindered access to the presence of God, not the absence of hard work among thorns and thistles. Just as dry soil becomes too hard for cultivation, so are the hearts of the first people; they became dry and hard without God. Perhaps Seth found the way to the source of living waters, and thousands of years before Jeremi-

> God's love for mankind never ceased, and He yearns to fellowship with us.

ah, heard God speak, "Call to me" (Jeremiah 33:3). The third son of Adam and Eve heard the same invitation, so he called, and he passed this calling unto his descendants Enoch, Lamech, and Noah. In turn, his descendants found their own calling and passed it onto those who believed and walked righteously before their God.

· LIFE LESSONS ·

ABOUT GOD. God is our Creator. He is the author of life. If we are here, in this century, this city, and this family, then it is not purely coincidental; it must be His idea and His divine purpose. He settled you here on purpose as if in your own garden, which you must cultivate, as it is part of His plan as well. And even when thorns and thistles grow in your garden, you must continue to cultivate by uprooting the weeds with the sweat of your brow. In time you will give birth to beautiful things, even through pain and suffering, as all this is part of life. And yes, there is a serpent somewhere nearby, like a roaring lion seeking to devour you, and yes, you have been given freedom, and every day there is a choice you have to make.

God is the Creator Who made us in His image and likeness; therefore, we, too, are creative beings—creative beings endowed with free will. So men have created centuries of endless warfare, hunger, misery, grief, and tears. Yet men can also create goodness, mercy, forgiveness, and love. Not only does our creative ability make us godlike, but also we understand our own responsibility for that which we have created; this is our desire for goodness.

ABOUT US. Every human bears God's divine supernatural life. God has breathed His breath of life into mankind. Life with God is described as "in Him we live and move and exist" (Acts 17:28 emphasis added) when He alone is our source of inspiration and strength. We take in—inhale His Life, and it renews and transforms us into the likeness of his Son Jesus, producing divine activity within us, unmistakably influencing everything we say and do. As we speak, we exhale. What is it that we breathe in and out of us? Each time you exhale, your words can influence your environment; our words can become a powerful force that brings forth life, recovery, and growth. **"The tongue has the power of life and death, and those who love it will eat its fruit" (Proverbs 18:21).**

ABOUT LIFE. In life we all have to do things for the first time. And we become greatly inspired by the examples set by those who have come before us. But what if we are pioneers—if there are no footsteps in front of you, if no one came this way before you? Who do you take your example from? Who can understand the difficulties of your path? Who can help you?

In any situation and in any circumstances, there is One Who has passed this way before who can be compassionate and able to help those who have fallen into temptation **"Let us run with perseverance the race marked out for us, fixing our eyes on Jesus, the pioneer and perfecter of faith" (Hebrews 12:1–2).**

ABOUT OUR NAME. What is my name, and how do I call myself? Perhaps after some events, mistakes, injuries, or disasters, we also were given a name that had a meaning. Or maybe there's an adjective affixed to my existing name—"that kind" Maryann, Sveta, Natasha. Sometimes people give nicknames to us that don't do us justice. It is completely unnecessary for you to take on and live up to the name that people made up for you. Yes, none of us are yet perfect, but the real truth about who we are is how God sees us. Now He sees us solely through His love, he looks at us as His beloved children, regardless of our age and no matter what we have done in life. **"See what great love the Father has lavished on us, that we should be called the children of God"** (1 John 3:1).

ABOUT PARENTING. What do we say about our own children, and what do we proclaim over their future? What do we call them? God says that children are a blessing and a reward from Him. Most of us wholeheartedly agree, and we wait for the birth of our babies with profound gratitude. As parents we have only the best of intentions for them, hoping to instill in them the love for both God and people, so that they are happy and loved. Nowadays, not many people give their children names with a special meaning, but apart from naming the child, we often refer to children by using common nouns and descriptive adjectives. Keep in mind that as life goes on, children can embody these nicknames, and many will become what their closest people see them as being. What an enormous responsibility that is! **"Do not let any unwholesome talk come out of your mouths, but only what is helpful for building others up according to their needs, that it may benefit those who listen"** (Ephesians 4:29).

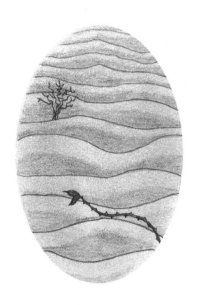

6

HAGAR.
ANGUISH MISDIRECTED

I vividly remember our first "honeymoon" after our children were born. Six years of marriage, four years in a new country, three kids—we were both working hard and slowly adjusting to our new way of life. My sister Anya was getting married, and we all flew back to Moscow for her wedding. My other sisters took care of our babies and sent my husband and I to the shores of the Red Sea—off for a week of vacation in Egypt.

While we were there we bought ourselves a tour, a trip into the desert on four-wheelers. We boarded a large air-conditioned tour bus and drove far from the city. When we got off the bus, the sun was straight over our heads blazing hotter than on the beaches. All the tourists began to tightly wrap their heads with traditional headgear, the black-and-white or red-and-white checkered scarves, and at first the whole scene looked ridiculous to me. After a very short briefing our caravan of twenty ATVs slowly moved into the vast expanse of the desert, passing by a couple of brownish hills.

Beyond lay barely noticeable tracks of the trail that were made by the same bikes the day before and nothing else but the strong wind stinging me with a million grains of sand thrown at my uncovered face. My kidneys and my entire body were made keenly aware of the absence of the usual pavement, so I gripped the steering wheel even tighter with both of my hands. I was driving behind my husband and used his back as my reference point. I tried to yell, but my voice was no match for the sound of the engine, and the wind blew my words to the side while generously adding a heap of sand to my mouth. *Thanks, but no thank you. I think I got enough of this desert experience; it is hot, windy, and full of sand. Can we now go back, please?*

> What would I do if I was lost here? What if I had my kids with me? What do I even know about surviving in the desert? Nothing.

As we drove farther and farther from the parking lot, the landscape looked stripped, void of any landmarks, not a single building on the horizon, no hills, not even a single tree. This was about ten years ago; back then we already had mobile phones, but there was no such thing as international roaming available. In my mind, of course, I understood that we were in the twenty-first century and we couldn't get lost here—after all, we had tour guides, the route had been checked out, and soon we would be back lying on the beach, and in a few days, we would fly back to our children. Nevertheless, spending these few hours bouncing on the ATV in the middle of nowhere left me feeling anxious and uncertain. We made a brief stop to pass out bottled water and to freely enjoy the surrounding scenery. But honestly, you didn't even have to look around. No matter where you turned, the horizon was the same: flat vastness covered by hot sand that would suddenly whip up to form dust clouds blown by the gusts of wind.

Just then I thought, *What would I do if I was lost here? What if I had my kids with me? What do I even know about surviving in the desert? Nothing. I only know a Bible story about Hagar and Ishmael. I also remember the extraordinarily colorful way Antoine de Saint-Exupéry depicted the desert.* This famous author was a pioneer of his day, a mail delivery pilot who had flown over the desert many times. He lived on a remote desert outpost and even survived a plane crash in the Sahara desert.

This must be the reason why we call the difficult periods of our life, times of adversity and suffering, metaphorical "deserts." The only difference is that real deserts are usually away from cities and towns and lie far beyond the fields and forests. Yet many find themselves in their personal desert among scores of other people, while in church, and even as part of large families. Unfortunately, we don't hear or even recognize the silent screams of these thirsty souls who have dried up without God's love.

Our friends will often say, *I am here for you*, and we ourselves may say it at the end of phone conversations, meaning *I'm here, call me. I am ready to help with anything you need.* But it is becoming apparent that the web of social media has entangled us all in a world of instant access and communication. We have become closer than ever, yet far removed at the same time. We are constantly bombarded by instant news updates while countless people suffer alone, and there's no one to hear their pain.

Ask a question on Facebook in a group "Russian Mama USA"—What dress should I wear or how to treat a common cold—and in just a few hours, hundreds of people will give you their advice. Ask a more poignant question, and there will be hundreds more comments and suggestions. Thus we tend to get the false impression that we are surrounded by caring people who are willing to help us.

But too often this is completely untrue, and frankly, the person in need will find themselves overrun by endless talk, empty advice, and useless information that cannot help them. The answers you seek simply can't be found there—because you are knocking on the wrong door. Sometimes the advice you'll get is just pointless—everyone knows everything about everything—but none of it is helpful.

Well, all you can do is pray, we then say or hear it said to us as we throw up our hands. What does this phrase even mean? The Lord says, "Call unto me" (Jeremiah 33:3). Nevertheless, when having done all they could, people sigh and say, *Well, there's nothing we can do now, except to pray.* Our humanity has reached the peak of its technological progress. Miracles can be created by modern medicine, and advanced technologies make it possible to accomplish almost everything we want by ourselves. We hardly ever need God anymore.

"My soul thirsts for you" (Psalm 63:1 NLT). We have been repeating the words of King David for so long, but most of us don't even know what thirst means. Honestly, we hardly ever experience any real physical thirst. Although everyone can become thirsty, and everyone can encounter a spiritual desert, few will walk through unscathed. Some will become lost and will remain in their desert forever. How can we find the source of water in the middle of the desert and escape it's torment? Where shall we call for help, where to look for the source that can save us and our children?

Early the next morning Abraham took some food and a skin of water and gave them to Hagar. He set them on her shoulders and then sent her off with the boy. She went on her way and wandered in the desert of Beersheba.

> When the water in the skin was gone, she put the boy under one of the bushes. Then she went off and sat down about a bow-shot away, for she thought, 'I cannot watch the boy die.' And as she sat there, she began to sob.
>
> God heard the boy crying, and the angel of God called to Hagar from heaven and said to her, 'What is the matter, Hagar? Do not be afraid; God has heard the boy crying as he lies there. Lift the boy up and take him by the hand, for I will make him into a great nation.'
>
> Then God opened her eyes and she saw a well of water. So she went and filled the skin with water and gave the boy a drink.
>
> God was with the boy as he grew up. He lived in the desert and became an archer. While he was living in the Desert of Paran, his mother got a wife for him from Egypt. (Genesis 21:14–21)

Hagar is a young, beautiful Egyptian woman. A bright girl with character, her life has only one major setback—she is a slave. This girl became a slave through an unfortunate sequence of events, and she must have tried her best to make peace with her new identity. Her masters are noble and elderly, a couple who have been on a lifelong journey to find a land that was promised to them by their God. They treat her very well, but a slave will always harbor hatred for her mistress—because of her, Hagar has been forced to leave the beauty of the Pharaoh's palace and her comfortable life and become a vagabond, a wanderer in the desert heat along with these peculiar Jews.

> She must have tried her best to make peace with her new identity.

Hagar still remembers the commotion that spread in the palace. Egypt, being rich and prosperous, was frequently visited by merchants from different countries. It seemed that nothing could surprise or impress the Egyptians anymore. But there was a small group of nomads, the wandering Jews, that piqued everyone's interests. There were rumors about a woman of extraordinary beauty, and Pharaoh himself heard of her.

The palace had plenty of young beauties, but there was something special in this middle-aged woman, the way she graciously carried herself as she walked across the marble floors of Pharaoh's palace. It seemed as if Sarai was a born queen, meant for the palace and not for the tents or wandering in the desert on hot days and on cold nights. Pharaoh took Sarai into his palace, letting everyone else go with Abram, who called himself her brother.

However, strange things began to happen in the palace with Sarai's arrival. One night Pharaoh had a terrifying nightmare, then he ordered that Abram return immediately. It turned out that he was not her brother at all; in fact, he was her husband. Nevertheless, instead of punishing Abram by making him pay for his trickery and lies, Pharaoh greatly honored him with many gifts. Then the Egyptian nobles escorted them out of the country, letting them go free with all their possessions and gifts: with all their livestock as well as men and women slaves, including Hagar, who was forced to leave her beloved Egypt behind.

Serving her beautiful yet childless, thereby unhappy, mistress is not always easy. Both of her masters, Abram and Sarai, are somewhat odd. Sometimes it seems as if they are both losing their mind as they keep talking about God's promise and their numerous descendants, to whom will be given a mythical land to which they haven't yet arrived. It seems bizarre to be counting your future descendants being numerous like the sea sand while they do not possess a single grain of sand.

Sarai knows that her chances of becoming a mother are getting slimmer with every passing year. But her husband's faith, on the contrary, seems to grow bigger and bigger. So Sarai decides to speed up the promise, and Hagar must become her master's concubine. Soon after, she realizes that she will become a mother to His Son.

Young, beautiful, and pregnant slave girl versus her mistress—also gorgeous, but an aging and childless woman. One is powerless, yet carries a lot of pride and her master's baby son in her womb. The other has all the power mixed with pride and envy. She will not allow her slave to display superiority over her. Hagar thinks that she is expecting a baby? No, it is Sarai who is expecting Abram's child from her slave. The maidservant is nothing but a surrogate. Just a few more rude glances and a few words exchanged between the two women—and pregnant Hagar finds herself lost in the desert.

Her gods are gone; the river Nile doesn't flow in this desert far from Egypt. *What if the God of Abram and Sarai lives in this desert? Maybe He is the God of the nomads maybe he can hear me? Maybe I should try and pray to Him?*

And the Angel of the Lord found her at the well of water in the wilderness and He commanded her to return to her mistress and submit to her (Genesis 16:7, 9 paraphrased). Hagar returned and gave birth to a son when Abram was eighty-six years old. She called him Ishmael, just as the angel had instructed her.

But Hagar's spiritual wilderness is not over.

Thirteen years later, God appeared to Abram as the Lord Almighty, and God made a covenant with him and changed his name to Abraham, "the Father of many nations." God also changed his wife's name to Sarah, which means "Princess." A year later, on Abraham's one-hundredth birthday, they witnessed a great miracle: Sarah gave birth to a son, Abraham's heir, as God Himself had promised. And they named him Isaac.

Plan A has been successfully implemented; hence, there had been no need for Sarai's Plan B. Having Hagar bear Ishmael was simply a mistake, a hasty decision. In hindsight, the slave woman and her son should have been more careful in this situation. But Ishmael, who has been spoiled by his father, unfortunately makes fun of baby Isaac during a holiday in his honor. After that misstep by Ishmael, several unpleasant conversations take place: Sarah has a word with Abraham, Abraham has a word with God, and finally, Abraham has a word with Hagar. Hagar and the firstborn are cast out.

Ishmael has been overshadowed by the promised child, Isaac, so, the Patriarch will continue on his journey to the promised land together with his wife and her baby without encumbrances. Fourteen years after her first desert experience, mother and son are right back—lost in the desert of Beersheba.

Abraham was a very rich man, but he did not give them any of his property, not a single animal, no camel, and no guide. He gave them enough food and water for just one day. Yet he did this not out of stinginess, but in obedience to God's command. God had said that He would take care of the boy Ishmael and make him a great nation. By then Abraham had already learned to fully trust in the Lord.

Now this woman and her teenage boy are lost in the desert of Beersheba. What does it even mean to be lost in the desert? To lose your way, to lose sight of any landmarks, to wander around in circles when you are running out of strength and there is no more food or water left. You begin to lose hope that you will make it out alive, and with every hour under the blazing sun, hope evaporates just like the water in your container.

But she can't give up. *There have to be wells here somewhere, an oasis with water. Somewhere here there must be roads traveled by caravans. How long can we keep walking in this heat?* They are both losing strength and they have nothing to replenish it with. Hagar's head fills with memories; thoughts flash through her mind. *I need to remember how I got out of the desert fourteen years ago. Yes, there was an angel. The Lord sent him; he commanded me to humble myself and return to Sarah. He told me that I would give birth to a son and promised that a whole nation would come from him. What was that all about? Was I hallucinating or dreaming? It would have been better for me to die then, when the child was still in my womb. It is unbearable to see my beautiful boy now, to see his future perishing, our life and our hopes fading away.*

Hagar leaves her exhausted son under the shade of a small bush and walks few hundred feet away from him. Sitting next to him listening to his labored breaths, wondering if each one is his last, seeing him fall into unconscious deathly sleep is beyond horrifying. And so his mother leaves him alone and walks off mumbling the same phrase over and over, "I do not wish to see my boy's death." She sits down at a distance and begins to weep.

What are her tears about? She is crying over her own fate, over her past and future. Her past was filled with injustice from the moment she was sold into slavery. When she was taken from the luxurious palace of the Pharaoh and given as a maid to Sarah, she was forced to roam the desert with them. She was mistreated by her mistress Sarah, who had given her to her own husband and then envied her for becoming

> Her soul, like the landscape all around her, feels parched and empty. Her bitter cry of resentment, anger, and hopelessness sweeps across the desert landscape, echoing to the north and the south, to the east and the west. Why?

pregnant. *Ishmael was just a spare for them; they only needed him in place of Isaac. They simply used me, then tossed me away!* She could at least understand why Sarah was envious, but Abraham—*How could Abraham exile his own child into the desert with only a day's supply of food and water?*

Suddenly a wave of self-pity rushes over her, leaving no room for self-reflection, repentance for her pride, or any remorse. There is just bitterness, victimhood, and self-pity. Bitter tears run down her cheeks. Her soul, like the landscape all around her, feels parched and empty. Her bitter cry of resentment, anger, and hopelessness sweeps across the desert landscape, echoing to the north and the south, to the east and the west. *Why? Why me? Why my son? Is there no justice?* But there is no one there to hear her screams. Hagar's anguish is misdirected. She is mourning her future. Their fate, both hers and that of her only son, looks utterly grim.

Fear is faith in the negative; it brings forth the very dreaded fate and misfortune that it fears. Hagar is in horror of their impending doom because the only future she can see for herself and her son is death. Her strength is gone, she has searched for water all around, but there is none. There is no one here to help them and no escape. She remembers how, just days before, as she looked at her handsome young boy, her beautiful son, Hagar dreamed of her own grandchildren and a large family that Ishmael would lead. Now he lies exhausted under a bush, and she is afraid to come any closer; she doesn't want him to overhear her cries. This is her anguish, one woman's suffering—a mother's heartbreak.

But she was aiming her cries completely in the wrong direction. Her cries of anguish were misplaced because she was self-absorbed; her screams were completely misdirected.

But help came because of the cries of the boy Ishmael. His father, Abraham, had taught his son how to pray. The voice of the boy was heard on high because Ishmael asked for help from above; his cry was directed toward heaven. Ishmael had faith in God, and in response to his faith-filled pleas for help, God sent His angel to Hagar.

She must have thought that she was hallucinating, being in distress, and awaiting her own death, when suddenly her old acquaintance showed up. He had spoken with her before and in very similar circumstances—in the same hot desert, only fourteen years before.

And just as back then, he seems not to notice the obvious and asks very strange questions. This time, the question he poses to this heartbroken and downcast woman sounds extremely out of touch and inappropriate: "What is the matter with you, Hagar?" (Genesis 21:17 NASB).

Look around, can't you tell what's going on here? Can't you see a woman is lost in the desert? Her lips are parched and blis-

> The voice of the boy was heard on high because Ishmael asked for help from above; his cry was directed toward heaven.

tered, her eyes dried up from crying. *Are you that blind? What troubles me?*

And in response to her blank stare, the angel says, "Do not be afraid; God has heard the boy crying as he lies there" (Genesis 21:17).

Do not be afraid! Fear paralyzes; it blinds us, preventing us from seeing the way out. Fear will overflow your soul, displacing any hope of salvation.

The angel does not wait for her reply, but calls her to action. "Lift the boy up and take him by the hand," he says. She gets up and does so, and just like that—her fear is gone.

Instead of retelling her whole ordeal; the hopelessness of her terrible situation, describing it all in colorful details, she simply did what the angel told her to do. Hagar arose, and as a consequence of her obedience, fear left her, and then a miracle took place! Suddenly she was able to see what was there all along but had been covered up by the veil of her tears, her bitterness, resentment, and fear.

God had opened up her eyes, and she saw a well of water.

Hagar had cried over herself bitterly for so long that it was as if she was standing in a room full of mirrors, perceiving a distorted reality. All around her she saw her own reflection—resentment, self-pity, fear, and hopelessness was her own self-image. And in the very center of it all was herself, a poor and miserable girl.

Crying for help in the wrong place—misdirected pitiful anguish—answers you only as an echo; it will repeat your own words back, doubling your troubles.

But an upward cry, a heaven-focused prayer, will not repeat your own words. God will hear on high and will bring you the answers you seek. God will show you the source that will become your salvation from doom, not only to you but to your children as well.

The answer came to Hagar as soon as she stopped crying over her poor self, as soon as she got up and began to act.

In Luke, chapter 21, Jesus tells his disciples about the end of time and all the terrible events that will come: famine, wars, and disasters. This can be described as the punishment humanity as a whole deserves. The Lord not only warns us that it will be grim, but He shows us the evacuation route far in advance. So what shall we do? It says, *When all this starts to happen, immediately send messages to all your friends by publishing posts on all social media platforms. When a new president get elected, begin discussing the topic of the coming of the Antichrist. Start investing in real estate in Arabia or, at the very least, move to Canada.* Right?

No. Instead, He says, "Look up and lift up your heads, because your redemption is drawing near" (v. 28 NKJV). Look heavenward. Yet every day, from north to south, from east to west, millions upon millions of times, there is an outcry—the sound of the cry for help. And yes, of course, we are called to help those in need and to stand up for the victims. Still, we are only His hands; He is the Savior delivering us from hell and death.

"My help comes from the Lord, the Maker of heaven and earth" (Psalm 121:1–2).

Help does not come from some powerful official, but from He Who made heaven and earth, Who created them from nothing. And He says, "Call on me in the day of trouble; I will deliver you, and you will honor me" (Psalm 50:15).

The prophet Jeremiah speaks from the Lord, "Call to me and I will answer you and tell you great and unsearchable things you do not know" (Jeremiah 33:3). You have no idea how close help is to you. You just can't see it yet.

Don't complain about your fate. Don't just cry for nothing. Don't mourn your past, don't weep fearing your future, don't look for help in all the wrong places, and do not look to people as your source.

> Look up and lift up your heads, because your redemption is drawing near.

Today we only have our present; our past and our future are out of reach. Now, today, God is here, and He is here right next to me. The One Who can open up my eyes is here. We think that we are seeing life as it truly is, that we are assessing what is happening around us correctly. But when God begins to open our eyes, then suddenly we begin to see "wells of water," and they appear within our reach because they were there all along. Every desert hides the springs of water that God means for us to find.

Lift up your heads.

Look up.

Blessed are those whose strength is in you, whose hearts are set on pilgrimage. As they pass through the Valley of Baka [Weeping], they make it a place of springs; the autumn rains also cover it with pools. (Psalm 84:5–7)

• LIFE LESSONS •

ABOUT GOD. God always hears those who turn to Him. He begins to open our eyes to show us His resources in response to our call **"Call to Me and I will answer you, and show you great and mighty things, which you do not know" (Jeremiah 33:3 NKJV)**

ABOUT US. Don't lose yourself in the same desert twice. If we fail our test, it will mean that we will have to do it again. Our everyday troubles, temptations, and difficulties are nothing but part of our human existence. Some may choose to run away from difficulties; others will choose to overcome them and pass their tests, going higher and higher. **"Blessed is the man who endures temptation, because, having been tested, he will receive the crown of life, which the Lord promised to those who love him" (James 1:12 oant).**

ABOUT LIFE. We need to learn to aim our grievance to the proper authority. Otherwise, all our crying will fall on deaf ears. Doors open to those who knock, and those who seek find. Unfortunately some people are used to making a lot of noise with nothing to show for it. Remember when the disciples of Jesus asked Him to teach them how to pray. The very first words of the Lord's Prayer direct our aim upward at Him, the giver of love and every good thing. **"Pray in this way: Our Father in heaven!" (Matthew 6:9 oant).** That is the correct address.

ABOUT PROMISES. God left literally hundreds of promises for us believers. Together with salvation and the gift of eternal life, He promised blessing in every area of our lives. They are all written on the pages of our Bible, all for us and for our children. But you can only get the promise by accepting it by faith. Take hold of the promise and rejoice over the future; stop imagining horrible things based on your circumstances. Try to imagine that which is promised to you, and it will begin to come to pass.

"Now faith is the assurance (title deed, confirmation) of things hoped for (divinely guaranteed), and the evidence of things not seen [the conviction of their reality—faith comprehends as fact what cannot be experienced by the physical senses]." (Hebrews 11:1 amp)

ABOUT SELF-PITY. Nothing is as blinding as self-pity; it robs us of the opportunity to seek a way out. Constantly mourning over your past or your future will not help you find your way out of the problem. The source of water may lie very close to the thirsty man. **"There is a way that appears to be right, but in the end it leads to death" (Proverbs 14:12).** Self-pity is exactly this kind of way—a dead end.

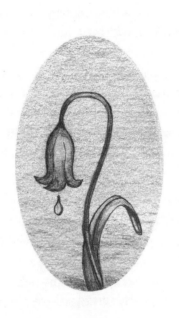

7

SVETA. THE BRIGHTNESS OF HER SOUL

My husband is a pastor. I have seen a lot over our years of following God and ministering to His people in the local church. We took part in many wonderful events and celebrations. Witnessing young couples becoming one through God's love, we have celebrated many beautiful weddings. Then, a few years later we would celebrate the couple's new arrivals. We would visit new moms in the birthing center, and then, together with our whole church, we would dedicate their babies to the Lord. We felt greatly honored to do these things.

There were also countless heartfelt conversations, which, sometimes lasted long into the night, counseling moments,

> Unfortunately sometimes the dark days visit our closest friends, leaving us powerless to stop the onslaught or carry their pain for them. All we can do is walk alongside them on their journey.

and prayers offered for those who were in trouble. Many times we would stand in the gap for those who were under attack with prayer and often with fasting. Still, life has different seasons, and so does ministry. There are workdays, holidays, conversations, corporate prayers, weddings, birthdays, and sometimes there are funerals. Unfortunately sometimes the dark days visit our closest friends, leaving us powerless to stop the onslaught or carry their pain for them. All we can do is walk alongside them on their journey.

In all these years, perhaps one of the hardest and most painful things for me was placing an order for a small newborn-size casket for our closest friends' baby boy. I stood in the funeral home of a small town, Camas, Washington, flipping the pages of the laminated brochure. I was choosing a grave plaque and the letter font that his name and date of birth would be written in. Just one date—his birthday, the day of his death.

Just a few years before that dreadful fifteenth of March, Sveta and I were secretly hoping that God would bless both of us with another child. One of us was a little under forty, the other a little over forty. We both already had kids, all in school and almost all teenagers. All our kids were wishing for a baby sibling as well. Sveta and I regularly saw each other at church, at least twice a week, and sometimes we got to discuss our little secret, lifting each other up and encouraging one another to trust the Lord, to be grateful for what He had already given us.

I remember when Sveta first told me about her pregnancy. We all were overjoyed for them. Time flew by; days turned into weeks, neatly stacking into groups of seven; weeks turned into months. At twenty weeks, at the long-awaited ultrasound, our friends found out that they were expecting a boy. Then came the third trimester—it is always more fun—time to pick out the crib and lots of other little things for the new baby. Every day their family would pray, giving thanks to God and praying a blessing over both mom and baby. Sveta's pregnancy was textbook perfect, no complications, and not a single reason for any kind of worry.

One Wednesday evening a few weeks before her due date, Sveta walked into our house wearing a gorgeous white gown revealing her perfectly round pregnant belly. This was her day—her party, her baby shower. Over thirty friends came to bless her by praying God's blessing over her pregnancy and upcoming delivery. Many of the girls knew how much this baby was wanted, and this party was full of love, joy, and genuine gratitude.

Now I am standing in the hallway of PeaceHealth Family Birth Center of Southwest Medical Center in Vancouver, Washington. We live in this city; our two youngest children, Pavel and Ariana, were born right here in this hospital on the same first floor.

I am trying to shake myself free from what is happening behind the doors right in front of me, searching my mind in an

> I am trying to shake myself free from what is happening behind the doors right in front of me.

effort to remember which rooms I stayed in back then. I try to remember but I can't; my thoughts are all tangled in my head.

I then try to remember how many of my friends have given birth in this hospital in the last ten years. I count at least twenty. Those were some of my favorite visits, holding balloons and flowers, and of course, I had a photo taken with each new baby for a keepsake. Everyone knows that I simply adore babies, and everyone would gladly let me hold their precious bundles who were only a few hours old.

Never could I ever imagine such a painfully terrifying visit to a family birth center as this one. *No, I refuse to believe in the reality of what is happening tonight. No, just don't think about the bad stuff, just keep praying and keep believing in a miracle—keep believing that Sveta will give birth to a living baby.*

Still standing by the wall, I look at the other end of the corridor. There are wide double doors to the operating room (OR) at the end of the hall. Mothers who have delivered their babies via C-section are wheeled in and out on gurneys, gently cradling their bundles of joy. I fall back into my memories.

* * *

I had my first C-section back in Russia in 2004. Back then it was done under general anesthesia, and the first day after the birth was a complete blur; I was dazed and in so much pain. My precious baby girl had been taken away from me and placed somewhere else, without me even seeing her. All I remember is pain and a feeling of terrible longing for her.

I remember what a wonderful surprise my C-section in America was, with epidural anesthesia. The date for our son Paul's birth had been set in advance, and in the last month of pregnancy I walked around already knowing the day and even the time of my baby's birth. Because of my past complicated eye surgery, every one of our three kids were C-section babies. It took me a long time to accept this about myself; what kind of woman was I if I could not experience a real childbirth? But after witnessing a twenty-four-hour-long natural birth of a family member and seeing the whole process up close, I finally relented and no longer regretted not giving birth naturally.

Early in the morning on the day of scheduled C-section, my husband and I arrived at the hospital, filled out last minute paperwork, and changed out of our street clothes. Then we snapped one last photo with my tummy before I was taken back to the operating room. My husband courageously walked next me holding the camera in his hand (back in "stone age" before smartphones). Back in the OR, doctors and nurses together with the anesthesiologist all joked around and carried

> Back in the OR, doctors and nurses together with the anesthesiologist all joked around and carried on like nothing important was happening; for them, there was nothing sacred here, just another ordinary workday.

on like nothing important was happening; for them, there was nothing sacred here, just another ordinary workday. *Come on people, something very important is about to happen here—my son is about to be born!*

I lay fully awake, but I didn't feel any pain, my body felt numb just below my chest. My husband was allowed to see what was happening behind a small curtain separating me from the doctors, and in just a few minutes, the doctor lifted a tiny, bluish, rounded ball with the umbilical cord still uncut right before my very eyes. The next few seconds seemed like an eternity. I jerked my head right out of anesthesiologist's hands, and asked about sixteen times a second, "Is he breathing? Is he breathing? Is he alive? Is he okay?"

The nurses had a good laugh at my reaction. The doctor was finishing his job by stitching me up, and my son lay wrapped up like a little ball right next to my face. I firmly held these precious six pounds, needles and wires sticking out of my hand, and I cried for joy. The anesthesiologist offered to snap a picture with our newborn. Even now as I look at these photos, I have tears in my eyes—these must be the deepest emotions a woman can ever experience.

* * *

A nurse comes out of the room and pulls me from my memories back into reality and the sole reason why we are here today. She asks if I want coffee. My eyes are burning; this dreadful morning began at three with a phone call from our friends, exactly twelve hours ago. I knew that Sveta is full term at forty weeks, and usually we get a call asking us for prayer when someone is going to the hospital to give birth. But from the first seconds of this phone call, we realized that something was terribly wrong.

The next five minutes after hanging up the phone my husband and I were praying as we dressed while trying not to wake the children. We wrote a few notes and put them in their rooms as well as in ours on the floor, in case they wake up without us there. It took fifteen minutes to get to the hospital. On the way I sent messages to close friends from our church, "Sveta is at the hospital, please pray right now!" We were on our way hoping to lift them up in prayer and to believe with them. We prayed and we believed that, miraculously, everything would be okay. It is three in the afternoon now. A nurse, who turned out to be Russian-speaking and even from our own hometown, tells me that Sveta will give birth to her dead son any minute now.

I look again at the end of the long hallway. Suddenly the wide doors of the OR swing open, and a large group of doctors and nurses begin to walks toward me, in between them a young woman on a hospital gurney holding a baby in her arms. Walking next to her is a tall, skinny, funny-looking young man in glasses who probably did not see himself in the mirror today because he is dressed in funny-looking disposable blue scrubs and an odd blue hat. A wide smile is stuck on this young father's face as his eyes go from baby to wife, barely keeping up with the nurses rolling her to her room. The group walks by just a foot from me.

Just for a minute or two, as they walk in my direction and then are parallel with me, as they pass by and turn a corner, everything in my soul suddenly turns upside down.

It seems as if someone has made a painful, deep, narrow cut, and this pain allows me to see that which lies below, the essence of what is happening around me—the disparity of life. My exhausted mind and my raw nerves absorbed every detail of this new life, this celebration that just passed by me a minute ago. These young people in glasses are now in their room. Perhaps now the young man cautiously takes the child into his shaking hands and hesitates as he is overcome by emotions and tears; maybe now for the first time in his life, his heart is filled with true love and pure joy, the kind he has never experienced before.

But only a few yards from them, just behind the corner, our friends are in an exact replica of that room, and Sveta has just given birth to a baby boy. He looks healthy, a perfect baby with the terrible exception of one fact—his little body holds no life. A few hours ago his innocent soul departed back to God.

I can't hold back my sobs any longer, and I slide down the wall to the bottom of the floor in tears. I cry—no, I howl—

from the hollow, lonely feeling of not being able to understand this pain and suffering. *But what about Sveta? I want to be next to her... even though I am so afraid... but maybe I can help shoulder her unbearable pain, and maybe it might feel a tiniest bit lighter.*

The nurse calls us in, and we walk into her room. Sveta is holding her chubby-cheeked baby wrapped in a blanket. She looks at him with so much pain and love all at the same time. She has only a few minutes before they will take him away for an autopsy, so she is trying to memorize every little part of him, to capture in haste every feature of his beautiful face. He looks as if he is sleeping, only he is very pale.

I can barely contain myself, trying not to scream with all the power of my lungs and vocal cords. *Good God, please, I believe that everything is possible!* I take his tiny cold hand into mine and faintly whisper, "Sweet baby, please wake up!" And then four crying adults interrupt this deathly silence, and we begin to pray. My husband and I ask the Lord to give them strength, and then we hear them say through their tearful sobs, "Blessed be the name of the Lord. Even right here. Even today."

> My husband and I ask the Lord to give them strength, and then we hear them say through their tearful sobs, "Blessed be the name of the Lord. Even right here. Even today."

Just then I realize, in times of great joy or great sorrow, what lies hidden within our hearts becomes plain to see, and this is who we truly are. I had seen how humble people handle grief a few times in my life. They do not scream in rebellion against God, and they don't ask audacious loud questions; neither do they point fingers at the sky.

It seems that they are so filled with God that in these moments, when it seems humanly impossible that God could be near them, the Lord Himself embraces them from inside and out. This must be the reason why they do not lose their minds from grief, their souls don't break down, they don't fall into depression, and they don't become drunks. This truly is miraculous!

There were two long weeks before the funeral after Sveta was discharged from the hospital. A lot of people came to visit them at home. We didn't want them to be alone, but at the same time I tried imagining what must she feel like. *What if all she really wants is to be left alone? What if she really wants to shout, Please leave, everyone please go home; just let me be alone for a while? How long does it take to accept what has happened after an unexpected tragedy? And how much time does one need to come to terms with and to accept it? To be in the same house where the nursery is right on the second floor, right next to your son's room, how can you walk up those stairs and look at that door?*

A few more steps and just behind the door, there were freshly painted light gray walls, a new cradle, and a changing table with a chest of drawers where all the baby's things are, everything that was so carefully picked out with so much love and affection still there.

But now the cradle stands empty, and the cold, dark emptiness is trying to creep it's way into your soul.

Yet Sveta keeps the darkness and the emptiness at bay. She lit the light within her soul, the light that can chase away the darkness. She listens to this song over and over—"Thy Will," written by Hillary Scott in 2016 after she, too, had lost a child—and Sveta finds comfort and peace. *I'm not alone; others have gone this way with God's help, and so can we.* Sveta welcomes friends, who bring with them more than just hot meals, hoping to at least somehow ease Sveta's burden of household chores. She seats her guests at the table, and she feeds them and even shares some with the new family who have just recently arrived from Ukraine.

How can her heart contain so much? How can she think of others at a time like this, being openhearted and keeping up with the conversations, even inviting more guests into her home?

Sveta worried about her older children, her daughter and son, so concerned, praying that they would not harden their hearts and not harbor resentment against God. But I think there was no better way to help them than leading them by her own example, by walking it out through the spiritual valley of death and discovering the hidden wells of strength and comfort there. Through it all, their whole family kept repeating, "Blessed be the name of the Lord." I have witnessed them saying these words in the midst of their pain and tears, yet they were said with humility and trust in the Lord.

***

The cemetery in Camas has a special place, alongside a low white fence, dedicated to the burial of babies. I walked along reading the names, surnames, and dates. On many gravestones there was only one date. Stuffed animals and flowers had been left on these graves. My husband and I with our children were among the few participants in this sad ceremony, on this cold and rainy March day. Sveta and her family should arrive any minute. For three of our children, this was their very first funeral. They are good friends with Sveta's children, and they wanted to be here with them.

We stood under a small tent where chairs were prepared for us. Here in America even such sad events are organized very neatly and beautifully. I look at my kids and think, *This little white coffin almost completely covered by a beautiful bouquet of fresh flowers—in it lies the little body of their friend's brother. Do they even realize that?*

The kids are very anxious and they ask, "Mom, what should I say? What are the right words to say in this case?"

"I don't know," I answer. "Maybe there are no such words. Maybe we will just be here, just be with them."

A few minutes later we all stood together under the same tent in front of the little white coffin with a huge bouquet on top and a small rectangular grave below, neatly covered on all four sides by artificial green turf. We shivered from the piercing crosswind and rain and from our tightly held tearful sobs.

My husband, a pastor, spoke words of compassion. He spoke about our God Who is with us here and now. The God Who holds the whole universe in His hand is also the One Who is holding their little son now. And there will be a day when they all will be together again. But until then, they need to be able to withstand this separation. Leaving the questions unanswered for now, they must continue living with and for God. Today we all, their whole church family, are witnesses that they are able to bear the death of their baby boy. We are witnesses of the power of God in their lives, witnesses to the joy of the Lord, Who is the true comforter and the lifter of our heads.

Yes, this is a true story about my friend Sveta. Did I mention that her Slavic name, Svetlana, means luminescent, shining, bright light? But even truer is the story of the divine light within her. It keeps on shining even through the dark veil of tragedy by illuminating the deepest darkness of suffering and pain. This light still shines through her as she leads worship today, standing on the platform with a microphone, praising the Lord. As she raises her hands to heaven, to her good God, she knows that her baby boy is there waiting for her. And her bright soul still sings to the glory of God, Who brings light to the darkness.

> The divine light within her keeps on shining even through the dark veil of tragedy by illuminating the deepest darkness of suffering and pain.

· LIFE LESSONS ·

ABOUT GOD. Apostle John gives us the good news, the gospel, which is directly applicable to us in our life and circumstances. **"This is the message we have heard from him and declare to you: God is light; in him there is no darkness at all" (1 John 1:5).** Nothing and no one can turn this light off when we are hidden in God; in fact, we are now living in His light. In darkness we can easily become lost and wander off the trail, not knowing where we are or where to go next. But in God, in His light, we can continue with peace in any circumstance.

ABOUT US. Everyone experiences grief in her own unique way, but some will go through the testing, while others can be crushed under it's weight. No one can stand ready for calamity. As a rule, trouble comes suddenly and without warning; thus our reaction is proof of what we are filled with. Those who daily walk with God, who are accustomed to leaning on Him to find strength, comfort, and support in their ordinary, everyday life, will also know where to draw their strength from in times of trouble.
"If you falter in a time of trouble, how small is your strength!" (Proverbs 24:10).

ABOUT LIFE. Life is bigger than the sum of it's parts. It seems that we all mean the same thing when we say life, but life is much more than our temporal existence on this planet in this physical body. **"God has sent his Son to us, so that everyone who believes in Him will not perish, but have everlasting life" (John 3:16).**

Eternal life is a life with a capital L, and unlike our physical existence, it is both everlasting and ever more meaningful. **"If only for this life we have hope in Christ, we are of all people most to be pitied"** **(1 Corinthians 15:19).**

ABOUT THE VALLEY OF THE SHADOW OF DEATH. Fear dwells in the darkness of the valley, but the way to overcome fear is to go through the valley with God. As we read in the Twenty-Third Psalm of David, he himself being a brave man, does not brag about his own bravery, but instead he shares his reasoning behind his confidence. **"Even though I walk through the darkest valley, I will fear no evil, for you are with me" (see Psalm 23:4).** As we walk next to the Lord, we can see His light and His purpose even in the midst of the darkest of valleys. **"You, Lord, keep my lamp burning; my God turns my darkness into light" (Psalm 18:28).**

ABOUT PRAISE. We can tap into unsurpassed power when we praise and worship our God. Victory comes to us as we magnify His name, as we begin to release words of praise and gratitude to our God.

In the Old Testament, the Second Book of Chronicles, the twentieth chapter, we read the account of King Jehoshaphat leading his army to battle. His army was no match for his enemy, and judging from human perspective his situation looked hopeless. But the King had put the Levites—the vocalists and musicians—on the front lines, and as they began to praise the Lord, in response to their worship, God the almighty came down on their behalf. And together with the presence of the almighty God, victory came in the form of a miracle. The allied nations that had come together against the Jews suddenly became confused, and they literally slaughtered each other on the battlefield. Then God's people were left to collect the leftover goods, which they did for three whole days. The Bible says that God is **"enthroned in the praises of Israel" (Psalm 22:3 NKJV),** and the presence of the Lord will bring us victory. Even though our answers may not always come in the way we expect them, nevertheless, the Lord does not relent and we shall surely triumph in Christ.

8

ESTHER.
BEAUTY WITHIN

In autumn of 2008 in Portland, Oregon, we hosted a music concert for the band Imprint, and I took part in this event as a talk show host. Our invited guest for the talk show was an extraordinary young woman, Lika Roman, crowned Miss Ukraine 2007. When she came to visit the United States, she never missed the opportunity to talk about her unique experience. Many became fascinated with her persona and came to see what this tall, slender, brown-eyed beauty with gorgeous long hair looked like in person, but to everyone's surprise she attributed her beauty pageant success to God and would talk about Him instead of talking about herself.

Lika grew up in Uzhhorod, a small town in Ukraine, where she lived with her mother. When she was a teenager she became a believer, put her faith in God, and dedicated her life to His purpose. She was studying in the university, serving in the local church, working as a beautician, and praying. In her prayers she would ask God about her future. She was convinced that the brightness of God's love must be shown everywhere and at any cost. And as she was making other women beautiful on the outside, God was preparing her to showcase His beauty on the inside. The first step in this journey was Lika's invitation to become a contestant in a nationwide beauty pageant in Kiev.

> She was convinced that the brightness of God's love must be shown everywhere and at any cost. And as she was making other women beautiful on the outside, God was preparing her to showcase His beauty on the inside.

The next step was overcoming her own doubts, criticism, and confusion. Then the difficulty of preparing for the contest itself began, but she kept a constant prayer in her heart: *Lord, what am I here for? I want to be the salt and light for these girls here.* Lika's reasoning was *God must have given me this opportunity so that I can tell the other girls about Jesus.* She didn't even dare to dream about winning the competition because she knew that in pageants like these the winner has been purchased well in advance.

But that year it just happened that a new member of the jury flew in to Ukraine to judge this contest for the first time—the distinguished Julia Morley of beauty pageant fame, the chair of the Miss World Organization. It was she who would give the final word that swayed not only the other members of the jury but ended up being the deciding vote. "Look at this girl, number twenty-three; she is different from everyone else. Look at how she is glowing." The other jurors were equally divided on the winner, so it was Julia Morley's voice that was decisive in Lika's favor. New opportunities opened wide before this young girl, and her very first words as the newly crowned Miss Ukraine were words of gratitude to the Lord.

But what had convinced me of her inner beauty was not how beautifully confident she was on stage with the microphone. We just happened to be in the process of moving from one house to another at the same time that Lika came to visit Portland. We were moving on Monday. Honestly, it was a stressful time for us after weeks of getting ready for the concert and the talk show on Saturday, then Sunday church service, and us moving the very next day. On top of that, our other friends were still living in our old house, and we had three little kids, our oldest being only four and a half years old, so there was a lot of packing to do in a hurry.

Lika, despite being a guest in our home, helped us move our things together with everyone else. Once I saw a picture of Lika that was taken at the pageant in Kiev. She was wearing a long evening gown and adorned with a crown, her face and hair done by professional makeup artists. She looked beautiful. But her real beauty became plain to see as this tall, slender girl dragged our huge bags to our new house; the bags were stuffed with our blankets and pillows, some of which came tumbling out as she carried them from our truck.

Today Lika continues being socially active, participating in countless youth events. She travels far and wide speaking at youth gatherings and conferences. Her audiences are mostly college and university students, young men and women who have bought into today's overemphasis on physical attractiveness and superficial beauty. But Lika's message is all about what gives life its true meaning. She speaks about the beauty within, about the beautiful meaning our life can have after we encounter Jesus Christ.

Our oldest daughter already has an Instagram account, and occasionally, after reading Lika's new posts, Katerina says, "Mom, do you remember how Lika helped us move to this house?"

"Yes, dear, I remember," I answer. "She is truly a beautiful girl!"

There was another girl who became a contestant in a nationwide beauty pageant and unexpectedly to herself and others won the crown. We can read her story in the Bible. Could there be a girl somewhere in the world who hasn't heard the Cinderella fairy tale? Even if there are to be was such girl, she probably knows another similar fairy tale, a true classic where a pitiful orphan suddenly becomes a beloved princess, when her raggedy clothes suddenly turn into beautiful gowns and she gets transported from the gutter to a palace, from rags to riches. Girls love these sort of stories just as much as boys love action and adventure, risk taking, and medieval tales of courage.

One such, if I may say so, "fairy tale" is written on the pages of the Bible. But unlike a fairy tale this story is true; nevertheless, it is simply fabulously beautiful. A twisted plot that tells of love and courage, this account of one girl beauty and bravery, the story of Esther, is so unique, so exceptional that God set it apart in a separate book—one of sixty-six books of the Holy Scriptures. This is the only book of the Bible that does not mention the Lord directly by name; nevertheless, it is completely and all about Him, the story of the mighty God of Israel living within one delicate Jewish girl's heart.

This book is the story of the descendant of unwilling immigrants who becomes a queen who would then become an intercessor for her people. This is her predestined purpose and future, but that will come later. Meanwhile, in the year 586 BC, Esther is just a simple young girl, like hundreds of others, who lives in a foreign country after the complete annihilation of her homeland, Judea, and the survivors' Babylonian captivity.

> This book is the story of the descendant of unwilling immigrants who becomes a queen who would then become an intercessor for her people.

Seventy years of captivity have passed, and now many of the Jews have begun to return to their homeland—back to the poor and decimated Judea, where their cities lie in ruins and the olive groves and vineyards stand desolate, ransacked and cut down by their enemies.

Those who believed that God's dwelling place and their home was in Jerusalem—the Land of Promise—have returned. Times were hard for them; there were hostile enemies to contend with. Even with the king's permission to rebuild their city and the temple, Nehemiah and his people had to hold a sword in one hand and a pickaxe in the other while working on the walls. But the Lord was on their side; with His help they were able to overcome every obstacle. The walls were rebuilt and worship resumed in the Temple, and all those who remained in foreign lands began to pray toward Jerusalem. Some would travel three times a year to worship but only those who were courageously devout.

The large Jewish community thrives in the foreign land where they are no longer slaves. The people began building houses and planting vineyards, and many have started their own businesses, but even though they live far away, many have not abandoned their devotion to the Lord, the God of Israel. They worship Him and keep all His commandments. Mordecai is one of these righteous people. He is also raising his uncle's daughter. Early in life, Esther became an orphan, and Mordecai acts as both her father and her mother. The young girl, having suffered the loss of her parents, has become very attached to Mordecai. She deeply cherishes his kindness toward her and has repaid him with her obedience and humility.

But the book of Esther does not begin with her. It begins with a peculiar story of a strange rebellion in the capital city of Susa, right in the palace of King Ahasuerus, the magnificent and mighty ruler of the whole Persian Empire. He rules over twenty-seven states, spanning from India to Ethiopia. But his wife Vashti dares to publicly disobey his majesty's order precisely at the high point of the feast honoring the King's greatness and wealth.

The appearance of the queen was to be the culmination of this grand celebration, which lasted 180 days—yes, for six whole months. King Ahasuerus has shown all his wealth and the grand splendor of his palace to his warlords and chief rulers of all the provinces, and in the end, he wants to show off his most treasured possession—his gorgeous wife. No one knows whether Vashti has been too preoccupied with the feast for the women, which she has arranged in her royal house, or maybe she wants to show off her free spirit and independence, but she simply refuses to come before the king.

Apparently at that time and in that culture, her act of defiance was an egregious violation. Not only did she violate the palace etiquette, but moreover, she violated her civic moral duty. To us it may seem to be just a silly whim of a spoiled queen, but the king would have none of it. He was absolutely enraged, and her actions caused an emergency council meeting between seven Mede and Persian princes. It was apparent that the queen was not only gorgeous but also highly influential among the women of her kingdom. Urgent measures had to be taken to prevent the other women from neglecting their

> But even though they live far away, many have not abandoned their devotion to the Lord, the God of Israel. They worship Him and keep all His commandments.

husbands in a similar manner. Vashti could not remain as the first lady, and she was thrown out from the king's presence. She was no longer allowed to come before the king. She wasn't just fired; she was "deported."

After the celebrations had passed and all the guests had departed, the king's anger has died down. And Ahasuerus needs a new wife, so observers are sent all throughout the kingdom, their job was to collect beautiful girls as contestants for the most important beauty pageant—Miss Persia; the winner will become Mrs. Ahasuerus. The main criteria for all the girls is of course beauty, a flawless face and figure. But no one could suspect what a beautifully powerful soul can be hidden within one cute brown-eyed brunette.

Hadassah, Mordecai's cousin, is among the beauties who are taken and placed under the supervision of the royal eunuch Hegai. Like the others, she must undergo a yearlong preparation before being shown to the king. And from that moment on she began her transformation from Hadassah into Esther, a journey from being an alien orphan to becoming a royal queen. Servants worked on her image all year long. But her body was not the only thing being pre-

> Servants worked on Esther's image all year long. But her body was not the only thing being prepared. God was working on her heart and soul, preparing her to fulfill the mission He has entrusted her with.

pared. God was working on her heart and soul, preparing her to fulfill the mission He has entrusted her with.

It is highly unlikely that any of these beautiful girls came to be there of their own will, and I don't think Hadassah would have chosen this for herself, to forever forfeit the opportunity to marry and have children, never to be part of a real family, in exchange for the tiniest chance of becoming a queen. Most likely she, like all the others, will end up in the king's harem as one of his numerous forgotten concubines.

I wonder what was in Hadassah's heart as she began her twelve-month preparation for the meeting with the king. *Did she mourn her fate? Was she discouraged or defiant? As the old saying goes, better to be born happy than beautiful. But why can't we have both?* Mordecai had warned her not to tell anyone about her Jewish background. Imagine how much will power it would take to forget your own name, the name given to you by your beloved parents, to call yourself Esther and to respond to a name that is not yours. But she possessed a humble spirit, and she gained favor because of the way she carried herself. It must have been something special that made Hegai notice Esther, and she won his favor, which resulted in her being placed into the very best part of the women's house. She was given all the necessary oils and cosmetics to enhance her natural beauty.

Every day, Mordecai comes to the gate of the women's house, and every day Esther talks with him. She does not get prideful because of her position in the palace. She does not think that it is unnecessary to report to her cousin all about her affairs, although she could do so. *What man could understand the details of women's beauty treatments?* But it will be this habit of constant communication that becomes indispensable in saving her life as well as those of her people.

A year has passed, and it is time for every beauty to meet the king. They have but one chance to make an unforgettable impression—one night with Ahasuerus. The girls can ask for anything for this night, any object of jewelry, clothes, or fragrance. Each of them in turn says her farewell to Hegai; in the evening she will enter the king's chamber and in the morning will become a permanent resident in the house of concubines under the supervision of Shaashgaz, the royal eunuch. All but one will suffer this fate, the one that the king will choose to be his wife.

> The girls can ask for anything for this night. Each of them in turn will enter the king's chamber and in the morning will become a permanent resident in the house of concubines. All but one will suffer this fate, the one that the king will choose to be his wife.

[Esther] was taken to King Xerxes [Ahasuerus] . . . Now the king was attracted to Esther more than to any of the other women... So he set a royal crown on her head and made her queen instead of Vashti. (Esther 2:16–17)

The trumpet sounds—and at the king's command, a royal crown is placed on Esther's head.

The king himself may not have understood what it was that so attracted him to Esther. She was beautiful, of course, but all the girls in that palace were highly selected beauties. We know the title Miss USA usually goes to someone's Miss Small Town. But Esther's beauty was not only skin deep; her beauty was not only the result of beauty treatments. A beauty both on the inside and out cannot be achieved in a year's time. This kind of beauty is the result of a different kind of treatments, the harsh treatment of suffering and life in exile, the character-shaping treatment, and also that of humility and great hope in God.

> But Esther's beauty was not only skin deep; her beauty was not only the result of beauty treatments. A beauty both on the inside and out cannot be achieved in a year's time.

Her outer beauty resulted from her inner beauty bursting out.

"Beauty will save the world," Dostoevsky will write two and a half thousand years after Queen Esther, but his words are exactly about her. "Beauty will save the world, but only if it's good. But can it be good?" Esther's beauty was good.

The honeymoon was soon over. But their happily ever after never materialized. Every fairy tale must have a villain: Cinderella had the evil stepmother, medieval tales have the princess and the dragon. In the same way in this story, in the spot where

I would like to put a happy ending, the devilish Haman suddenly appears.

The time of harsh testing first comes for Mordecai, who stands out of the crowd like a lone lamppost when he will not bow before the noble Haman as he is passing by.

Mordecai understands the risks, but he cannot break the commandment "Worship the Lord your God, and serve him only" (Matthew 4:10). Haman would never even notice the lonely Jew standing daily by the royal gates, refusing to bow and worship him, but Mordecai has enemies, the guards at the gate who hated Jews.

For overambitious and arrogant Haman, his fast ascent and high position in the royal court feels a little not enough. And a lone standing, wretched Jew does not just upset him but whips his pride into an outrage, causing him to conjure up a genocidal plan of revenge.

> **Yet having learned who Mordecai's people were, he scorned the idea of killing only Mordecai. Instead Haman looked for a way to destroy all Mordecai's people, the Jews, throughout the whole kingdom of Xerxes. (Esther 3:6)**

Suddenly Haman's wicked idea is being neatly presented to the king, and the royal seal is slipped into the hands of Haman himself. Messengers are being rushed out to every state and province, to the very ends of the Empire with a decree stamped by the royal seal. The day of extermination of the people of God has been set and the countdown has begun.

But the young queen who lives in the palace is clueless about the unrest in her city. She has no idea that Mordecai is standing at the gate wearing sackcloth and ashes. Esther sends a message through one of her eunuchs, who brings her a copy of the royal decree about the impending extermination of all the Jews and Mordecai's plea for help: Go to the king, and beg him for mercy for our people (Esther 4:8).

No, no, Mordecai, you don't understand the customs here, you are not aware of the palace etiquette. So Esther returns the answer: It can't be done! "For any man or woman who approaches the king ...without being summoned ...[will] be put to death." (Esther 4:11). There is a single exception— only if the king extends his golden scepter toward the intruder, then he will remain alive. If only she could be sure of the king's attitude toward her. It seems that the mood of Ahasuerus is extremely volatile—he has not sent for her in thirty days.

Then Esther receives a second message from Mordecai. This time it is even more insistent and direct. He talks to her like she is still his little cousin Hadassah and not his royal highness. But that little girl has ceased to exist! Difficult questions are tormenting her mind. *Does he really think that I can make a difference here? I cannot cancel the king's decree—it is written in stone—the law of Medes and Persians is written forever. Does he really want to send me to a certain death?* "If you remain silent at this time, relief and deliverance for the Jews will arise from another place, but you and your father's family will perish" (Esther 4:13–14).

And then Mordecai says words that suddenly become plain for him to see, like the missing piece of the puzzle in this still-unfolding picture of his own life and in the twists in Hadassah's fate. "Who knows, perhaps you have come to your royal position for such a time as this" (Esther 4:14 HCSB).

These are harsh words from her cousin, but she still manages to hear love in them—love not only for her but also for their people. Her long-ago learned habit of obedience and her abilities to listen and see things through the eyes of other people help this young woman to make the most difficult decision in her life.

> Her long-ago learned habit of obedience and her abilities to listen and see things through the eyes of other people help this young woman to make the most difficult decision in her life.

My life is bigger than just me, I must be here for something bigger. Yes, it seems *the palace is a safe place—there are guards everywhere, and no one here knows that I am Jewish. Going to see the king without his invitation is a crazy idea, a gutsy step toward certain death. A woman like me—how can I make a difference for a whole nation?*

The king's decree has already been delivered to every city and all the regions; every nation is reading it now in their own native tongue. And the countdown has already begun—now it is only a matter of time. But on the other hand, what if I could?

"For such a time as this?" Could all this be God's providence? But was it not the king who has chosen me? Maybe I was simply his type? The Lord has His priests, His prophets and Levites—how can a simple girl be chosen to be His instrument to save His people? All these conflicting thoughts danced in Esther's head.

By this time Hadassah has already become Esther. But now is the time for Esther to become the queen and to take responsibility for her people. And she does it. "I will go to the king, although it is against the law, and if I perish, I perish" (Esther 4:16).

Three days of fasting before Esther goes before the king are observed by Esther, Mordecai, and all the Jews. The king extends his golden scepter to Esther; and she is saved from death.

But she still needs to save the Jews somehow.

Ahasuerus realizes he has missed his wife, and he generously offers to grant her desire, any desire up to half his kingdom. Yet the young woman does not jump for joy imagining dollar signs with many zeroes behind imaginary fortunes,

> Within the graciousness of her husband's extended hand and his outstretched golden scepter, Esther sees the hand of the Lord and the answer to the prayers of thousands of Jews.

nor does she have ambitions to launching her own fashion line of clothes; she does not daydream of what could have been. Within the graciousness of her husband's extended hand and his outstretched golden scepter, Esther sees the hand of the Lord and the answer to the prayers of thousands of Jews.

God gave Esther a wise plan—how she should approach the king with her request. So in response to her majesty's generosity she asked her king to grant her his full time and undivided attention. She invited her husband to come to her royal feast—along with Haman who had just recently been promoted—without uttering a single word of accusation or any pleas for help. This would be a feasting that prevented genocide, a bloodshed-canceling banquet.

The lady at the table turned out to be an excellent diplomat. An orphan girl had become a heroine and a courageous advocate for her people.

After the dust had settled and the countermeasures took full effect, the Jews had a new holiday to celebrate—Purim—and Mordecai became the second most powerful person in the kingdom. King Ahasuerus finally understood why he had chosen Esther to be his wife. All this time Esther's outward beauty was an outburst of her beautiful soul and the strength of her spirit within.

• LIFE LESSONS •

ABOUT GOD. Every one of us needs a Mordecai, someone who can advise, nudge, and inspire us to make the right choices. And every one of us has that quiet voice of our own conscience, the voice of the Holy Spirit prompting us what to do next. Often, other people will echo His guidance into our lives precisely because they also hear His voice. **"But when he, the Spirit of truth, comes, he will guide you into all the truth. He will not speak on his own; he will speak only what he hears, and he will tell you what is yet to come"** (John 16:13).

ABOUT US. Beautiful physical appearance is hereditary. But beauty can also be earned. Pedigree is unmerited, but the one who has gone through years of "treatments" working on her own character has acquired a different kind of beauty, the luminescent deeper kind. And every girl who will devote herself to taking care of her inner self can become a true beauty. **"Your beauty ...should be that of your inner self, the unfading beauty of a gentle and quiet spirit, which is of great worth in God's sight."** (1 Peter 3:3–4).

ABOUT LIFE. Life is bigger than we are, yet the spirit of our time is marked by selfishness, self-indulgence, stress avoidance, and constant comfort seeking disguised as inner harmony with oneself. A selfish life is full of emptiness, but a life of self-sacrifice, of being helpful and being needed by others, will fill our souls with meaning. **"Not looking to your own interests but each of you to the interests of the others" (Philippians 2:4).**

ABOUT BEAUTY. Inner beauty is captivating. "The one who is wise saves lives" (Proverbs 11:30), the wise Solomon wrote. **"Charm is deceptive, and beauty is fleeting; but a woman who fears the Lord is to be praised" (Proverbs 31:30).**

ABOUT TAKING RISKS. Everything in life comes with a price tag; the willingness to pay it is directly proportional to love. Esther loved her people so much that her attempt to save them was in her eyes worthy of her own life and destiny. What values do we hold dear, and what are we willing to risk for them? **"Greater love has no one than this: to lay down one's life for one's friends" (John 15:13).**

9

MARTHA. FEAR VS. FAITH

My mother never went to bed if my dad wasn't yet home in the evening. I think I must have inherited this useful but inconvenient habit from her. I remember how, after putting the children to bed, Mom would stay up and sew, wash, and iron heaps of linens while waiting for Dad to come home from his meetings or trips.

I always tried to help her finish the house chores so that there would be enough time left for her to sit down and make me a new skirt. All my favorite outfits in my childhood and in my youth were sewn or stitched by my mom from the clothes that came via humanitarian aid. I still remember the very first parcels from Sweden with shoes and clothes. The strange styles were not suitable for us to wear, but they were made with beautiful high-quality fabrics, and by adding her skilled hands to those clothes, Mom had all us children beautifully dressed.

One late autumn evening about ten years ago, I was waiting for my husband to return from a Bible college. Vasily was teaching in Tacoma, near the Seattle area, a little more than two hours away from us, or 135 miles. He taught there every semester. Class would end at 10:15 p.m., he would call me as he would leave, and by one o'clock in the morning, he was usually home. Our evergreen state of Washington is famous for rain from early fall to late spring. Living here, we don't mind the rain with one exception—driving in the rain at night.

That night, I had put the children to bed and, having finished all the chores, I decided to call Vasily, knowing that at the end of his two-hour trip, he was very tired, and talking to me would keep him awake. But my husband did not pick up his phone. Nor did he pick up the next five times I called. Silence, midnight, time slowed down as minutes stretched on and on, and nightmarish thoughts filled my mind, clashing with lightning speed.

At first I just kept calling and praying. When the small hand of the clock slipped past one o'clock in the morning, I stood near the window, attentively listening to every sound of a passing car in our neighborhood and fighting to keep the chill of paralyzing fear at bay. Why do we conjure up pictures of accidents and wrecked cars in moments like these? And if you lose the grip on yourself, you'll begin to cry spontaneously as if something terrible has happened.

At 2 a.m., not knowing what else to do, I called my parents in Moscow and asked them to pray. Then I woke my husband's elderly parents, knowing that high blood pressure and subsequent medication dosage would surely result from my call. But at that moment, I could not stand against my fear alone. I desperately needed to hear their prayers, to hear them say that my husband is in God's hands, the hands of our gracious heavenly Father. The words of their prayers would fill my soul with faith in God and trust again because fear has no place where there is faith.

> At that moment, I could not stand against my fear alone. I desperately needed to hear their prayers, to hear them say that my husband is in God's hands, the hands of our gracious heavenly Father.

Vasily never called me back. The battery on his phone had died, and he didn't have a charger in his car. He was exhausted, so he drove to the gas station, parked his car, and fell asleep for a few hours. He didn't think anything of it, so he quietly opened the door at three o'clock in the morning, trying not wake anyone up. Imagine his surprise when he saw me standing in the hallway and praying with his parents with the phone on speaker.

Oh, why do we stress, cry, and anguish over nothing? What a foolish thing to do! But what if the situation were different. Unfortunately, life can provide real reasons for fear and anxiety; on the other hand, we can needlessly worry stirring up our worst fears. And dare I suggest that I am not alone in this. It's not just one's natural inclination to worry about loved ones, circumstances, and situations. The problem is much deeper than that.

Humanity has an enemy who uses fear as a powerful weapon, and there is not a single person on this planet who is unfamiliar with the feeling. Surely, this is the reason why God tells us in His Word, "Do not be afraid!" numerous times. He not only says it but also shows us the path to victory—overcoming fear through faith. Faith in God is made evident through our trust in Him. The Lord Himself has promised to be our present help. Jesus says to Martha, "Did I not tell you that if you believe, you will see the glory of God?" (John 11:40). To believe means to have no fear.

> Humanity has an enemy who uses fear as a powerful weapon, and there is not a single person on this planet who is unfamiliar with the feeling.

Martha became a witness to a great miracle and God's glory. But before that, she had to face suffering, illness, and the death of a loved one.

Jesus had twelve apostles, seventy disciples, many followers, critics, enemies, and friends. Yes, He had friends in the usual sense of the word—good old friends, simple country folk at whose house he could stop by any time, get some food, and spend the night. The Gospels tell us the story of one such family. It was not the usual kind of family but an adult man and his two sisters. Early in life they must have lost their parents, and perhaps one of the sisters had made poor choices for her life; she might have been deceived or disappointed in love. But after meeting Jesus, her broken life and destiny were forever changed and not only hers but theirs as well.

Lazarus, Mary, and Martha lived on the southeastern slopes of the Mount of Olives in the little picturesque village of Bethany, practically in the suburbs of Jerusalem. This beautiful village was very close to Jerusalem and its magnificent temple, yet at the same time it was far enough from the hustle and bustle of the big city. Three times a year their village would be overrun with pilgrims coming from all around Judea, Galilee, and the remote parts of the Roman Empire. The crowds would come on high holy days to worship in the temple. Afterward Bethany would quiet down again, returning to its peaceful flow of rural life among the olive groves, date palms, and vineyards.

The main population of Bethany were Galileans. Many of them would host their fellow countrymen visiting the capital, merchants and pilgrims alike. In any city you can still find humble people who haven't forgotten their roots who will graciously host you in their home.

The Jewish oral tradition tells us that there were charity homes in Bethany, hospices and shelters for housing the poor and homeless. According to Jewish law, such homes had to be located at a distance of no less than three thousand cubits, or just under three miles, from the temple.

The word *Bethany* literally means the House of Affliction. That tells us that it was not an affluent community, yet Jesus loved to visit here during His ministry. It was also here on the mountain near Bethany that He ascended into the heaven after His resurrection.

> The word *Bethany* literally means the House of Affliction. That tells us that it was not an affluent community, yet Jesus loved to visit here during his ministry.

We read in the fourteenth chapter of Mark's Gospel about the house in Bethany of Simon the leper, who was healed from leprosy by Jesus. When Mary came to anoint the feet of Jesus with fragrant myrrh, it was also here in Bethany, and as his disciples scorned her, Jesus said, "The poor you will always have with you" (Matthew 26:11), as if pointing to their surroundings and silencing their disapproval.

We know very little about Mary and her sister from the Gospels. Lazarus may have been the oldest and as the male, following tradition, he replaced his father as the head of the family. He was kind, openhearted, and neighborly. He accepted Jesus with joy and faith and his home was always open to the Lord.

Lazarus carried the burden of responsibility for his sisters. He would worry about Mary, about her fate and reputation and about their future. Men are like that—they keep everything on the inside, they worry, and then suddenly they become ill. Sometimes they even die.

Martha and Mary are sisters, but they are so different. Martha is practical, active, and diligent; Mary is perceptive, mild mannered, and spirited. Martha is the good girl, compliant, doing what she must instead of what she wants. It looks as if she was the older sister and, therefore, the mistress of the house. In the Gospel of Luke, we read, "A woman named Martha opened her home to Him. She had a sister called Mary" (Luke 10:38–39).

Jesus did not came to the house alone; a crowd of hungry men came along with Him. Martha's first reaction as a gracious hostess was to start cooking and setting the table.

Perhaps she was a perfectionist, so the stale bread and leftover cold cuts with ordinary wine would not do for such honored guests. She began to prepare a grand meal. She counted on her sister to come and help her, but Mary was a no-show. Martha found Mary sitting at the feet of Jesus, listening to His sermon. Undoubtedly, the stories that Jesus was telling were profound and mesmerizing. Martha would not mind listening to them herself, but she was just too busy.

And then she had a brilliant thought, *Now is the perfect opportunity to teach my lazy sister a lesson. Of course, surely she will listen to Jesus!* And being granted this amazing opportunity to ask something of the Messiah Himself, out of everything one could inquire of Jesus, all her own needs and questions, Martha chose the following: "Lord, don't you care that my sister has left me to do the work by myself? Tell her to help me!" (Luke 10:40).

Jesus looked at her with profound love and sadness. "Martha! Martha! You are worried and upset about many things, but few things are needed—or indeed only one. Mary has chosen what is better, and it will not be taken away from her" (Luke 10:41–42).

Jesus did not tell Martha to leave the dinner alone. He did not tell her, *Come, sit, let's just talk, and then I will perform a miracle to feed everyone.* The Lord reproached her not for *what* she was doing, but for *how* she was doing it. Martha stressed and worried about an array of different things, but it is better to choose that which will count for eternity, that which cannot be taken away from you.

> Jesus did not tell Martha to leave the dinner alone. The Lord reproached her not for what she was doing, but for how she was doing it.

As someone who was conscientious, responsible, and hardworking, it was hard for Martha to understand the importance of what looked like laziness. Not only did she scorn her sister—who was all ears sitting in the company of men, completely forgetting her kitchen duties—but Martha was absolutely sure that Jesus would put Mary in her place, since He understood all things. But suddenly she heard a rebuke!

After the Lord reminded her about priorities, it seems that Martha did finish cooking that dinner. She fed them all, and as she was clearing the table, she probably wondered, *How do I prioritize my life to find that balance?*

Practical love expressed through serving others was Martha's love language. She said *I love you* to others through the clean clothes they got to wear, through the clean hose they got to live in, and through the delicious food they got to eat. Martha shouted *Amen!* every time she heard the story of how Jesus took pity on the hungry crowd of people and fed them. After all, God had created her this way; her Creator equipped Martha with these abilities and talents, and she expressed her love and devotion through them.

So what did the Lord mean when he spoke about Mary's choice? What is the gospel that extends life beyond death? The "better part" is when people are more important than dinner, when peace is more important than success, and when love and patience exceed our desire to impress someone with a gourmet dish. Feeding the spirit rescues us from eternal death; therefore, the soul is more important than the stomach.

* * *

Mary's story is not quite clear, and to us it will remain ambiguous. We read about Mary at a dinner party in the house of Simon. She anointed the feet of Jesus with fragrant myrrh and wiped them with her own hair. Yes, this was that exceptional case when all the respected men shuddered from contempt and silently scorned her. *If only He knew who she was.* In fact, they all knew her too well, and some of them intimately knew who she was and in this moment hoped and prayed that she did not remember their faces from that dark night.

One can only wonder what could have pushed a young girl from an ordinary family to fall so low. Whether it was grief from losing her parents that broke her heart or hopeless love or perhaps the man she loved and hoped to marry deceived her. One thing is certain: Most often, the woman who sells her "love" is a broken vessel, desperately searching for love, lonely and depressed, rejected by her own family. She is hated by the women in the city and despised by all the men, even those who have purchased the pleasure of being in her arms. A hollow and desperate soul is trapped within her beautiful body. Loneliness fills her eyes with seduction, but in the morning her bed is empty. Her lovers have gone home to their wives, leaving the emptiness that cannot be filled. Her heart is broken; like a vessel that has a crack, she is unable to contain anything at all within herself.

> In the morning her bed is empty. Her lovers have gone home to their wives, leaving the emptiness that cannot be filled. Her heart is broken; like a vessel that has a crack, she is unable to contain anything at all within herself.

Now Mary, like hundreds of other souls who are just as broken, hears about a man who is unlike any others. He can see through people right to their hearts and souls. He is the heavenly physician

Who has the power to heal. Given her diagnosis, she is desperate; left untreated, her fate is sealed, and shameful death awaits her now. But getting to see this man is not that easy. Besides her, there are thousands of people. He is surrounded by His fans and disciples, the sick, the lame, the lepers, the possessed, and hungry crowds of people. How can one get a moment of His attention? Who is going to let her near? Even the children are not allowed to be around Him.

But Mary knows her soul is gravely ill, she can't go on like this much longer; she desperately needs to show it to a doctor. Showing up uninvited during festivities at the house of Simon when he has invited Jesus with His disciples to dinner is a crazy idea. Her audacity as a disgraced woman is not without risk to her own safety. But when your soul is almost dead, your thirst for life is bigger than your fear. Mary takes a daring step. She walks into the house; the windows are full of light, the mouth-watering smells of grilled meat and good wine fill its courtyard, and the sound of men's voices mingled with festive music can be heard all the way down the street.

Suddenly all this is interrupted, voices are hushed, and the music falls silent. Dozens of eyes flare with anger, and faces contort in disgust as they see her. *How dare she!*

But Mary sees no one except Jesus. Her eyes meet His, and a sacred dialogue takes place amid this deafening silence, an in-depth heart-to-heart that only He and she perceive. Finally, she understands it all perfectly, awestruck by His forgiveness. She still holds the jar in her hand that she has brought as a

> Mary sees no one except Jesus. Her eyes meet His, and a sacred dialogue takes place amid this deafening silence, an in-depth heart-to-heart that only He and she perceive.

gift for Jesus. It is an extravagant offering, and his disciples could have sold it for a large sum; after all it is equivalent to a yearly wage. But Mary, overcome by her emotions breaks the jar and pours the precious fragrant myrrh on Messiah's feet. And the whole house fills with fragrance.

This was her outward expression of the inner healing taking place deep within her embittered soul, casting down every offense and stronghold, tearing to shreds everything that has been holding her captive. Her ice cold heart begins to melt; an enormous iceberg hidden within her tiny frame liquefies and rushes out from her soul as a flood of tears. Her tears flow and wash the dusty feet of Jesus as Mary wipes them down with her pride, her beautiful long hair. All of her is laid there at His feet with all her sins and fortitude, and so she lavishes her whole life's savings on Him without any regret.

When she stands up, the hushed sound of murmuring goes through the crowd of righteous men. Jesus spoke to them first and only then to Mary. His subtle words silence all her critics as proof that her offering has been accepted and so has she. Never has she encountered such a man before; His gaze sees right through her heart and soul, and for the first time in her life, she encounters true love—the kind that heals and accepts, the kind that gives you wings and brings life and hope.

* * *

This is Mary's story. *So how could I now be in the kitchen when Jesus Himself is in my house?*

Her place is at His feet; she has forgotten all about the food and about the people who need to be fed. She is after a different kind of nourishment, the heavenly bread that only Jesus could provide. Now that she has met Him, she is hungry for the things of the spirit, forgetting all about food.

Time goes by. Then comes trouble. Lazarus gets sick, deathly ill.

But surely there is nothing to worry about. After all we are personally acquainted with Jesus!

They have heard of countless miracles performed by Him. His ministry is becoming legendary, stories about Him are told in the town square and at the well. Everyone hears these stories at dinners as they are recapped by His disciples and even by Jesus Himself. Moreover, they could feel the supernatural power of God accompanying the ministry of the Galilean as they hear these stories themselves.

All we need is Jesus! Both Mary and Martha firmly believe that the answer is in Jesus. Their faith is strong and unshakable. *Lazarus, please be patient. We have sent for the Master already, and He will be here soon. Surely He will soon come to help as any true friend would!*

How many times have people asked Jesus for help—for themselves, for their relatives, their children, and even for their servants? Yet this is no ordinary request—"The one you love is sick" (John 11:3)—as if they are saying, *Jesus, You are constantly surrounded by crowds of people, the needs are so many, but this one is from your friends, the ones closest to You.*

Jesus receives the message "signed and delivered." But as Lazarus lies sick in Bethany, Jesus doesn't come. The "life flight" is delayed and not by a few hours but by several days. This strange delay is completely puzzling not only to the sisters who are expecting Jesus, but to His disciples as well. After three days, when Lazarus has died and is buried, only then does Jesus tell the disciples, "Now it's time to go. Lazarus is dead, but I am going to resurrect him" (John 11:11 author's paraphrase).

It seems that by his delay, the Lord wanted to once again illustrate that He has no favorites. In fact, His family and the closest to Him were those who surrounded Him then and there. Oh yes, He loved their family, He cared for them very much, but He came to introduce the whole world to His Love—incomprehensible, unmerited, and as yet undiscovered.

> It seems that by his delay, the Lord wanted to once again illustrate that He has no favorites. In fact, his family and the closest to Him were those who surrounded Him then and there.

Four days have passed after Lazarus's funeral. Martha hears that He is coming, leaves everything behind, and runs to see Jesus. She runs toward Him in tears, anguished and bewildered, full of resentment and doubt. Forgetting her place and formalities, she utters the first words. A lump of pain bursts out of her as a sharp reproach. "If only You had been here, my brother would not have died" (John 11:21 NLT).

Yes, she believes, she still believes that Jesus could have healed him. But she no longer believes that anything can be done now.

Jesus does not answer her reproach, He does not apologize, nor does He justify himself. He says, "Thy brother shall rise again" (John 11:23 KJV).

Martha has not forgotten her faith. She knows her doctrines well; her theology is still intact. "'Yes,' Martha said, 'he will rise when everyone else rises, at the last day'" (John 11:24 NLT). But the encouraging *then* does not stop her pain *now*.

He says to her, "I am the Resurrection and the Life..." But she cannot find comfort in these words because her brother is dead. "...He who believes in Me, though he may die, he shall live" (John 11:25 NKJV). And then He asks her the most important and very direct personal question, "Do you believe this?" (John 11:26 NKJV).

Could it be that Martha has already forgotten what has happened to Mary? Was she not spiritually dead, and didn't the Lord resurrect her soul and spirit?

"Yes, Lord, I believe" (John 11:27), she replies. And within her heart, she continues, *You are the God Almighty, You are an all-knowing and ever-present great God. But it's too late for us here and now. I know Who You are, but it has gone too far for any hope.*

Just then Mary comes, accompanied by a crowd of friends, and sorrow comes to Jesus, gripping even the Son of God, He begins to weep, seeing the people He loves in so much pain.

Jesus asks where Lazarus is buried and directs for the grave to be opened. Perhaps Mary watches with awe and reverence, but Martha... Martha believes so strongly in God Almighty, yet she also strongly believes that it is too late for them. Her logic and pragmatism are rooted in facts. Four days in the tomb. Her brother is dead. Jesus did not come in time. It is too late. Event horizon.

"Did I not tell you that if you believe, you will see the glory of God?" (John 11:40). Do not be afraid, only believe!

Why does Jesus speak to Martha about unbelief, which is really fear? Is fear the biggest obstacle to a miracle? Fear is unbelief—fear that nothing can be changed, that a miracle is impossible, or that it is true but just not for me. Nevertheless, fear and faith cannot coexist, and one can see the glory of God only if she has faith. One cannot say, *I believe in God Almighty, but I fear that a miracle is impossible.* These statements are mutually exclusive. God is either almighty, or He is not. You can either believe or be afraid. And every one of us has this choice to make.

And what of Mary? Mary has already learned to overcome her fears when she went to the house of Simon. All the men who gathered there were the nobles and saints—the dignitaries of her city and Jesus with His disciples. What if she was kicked out or worse, stoned to death? But she overcame her fear and came to Jesus with true repentance. And although she had full right to fear them, Jesus did not condemn her. Even as hatred poured on her from the eyes of the rest of the "righteous" men, He did not cast her out. And this was the main reason why: She did not come for them. Of course, she remembered how some of them came to her, but she came to Him, and her soul came alive with His love and acceptance. She has already witnessed the resurrection once—her own soul's resurrection. And Mary believes.

Mary, Martha, the disciples, the mourners, and plain onlookers—it is not only they who watch what is about to happen on the outskirts of Bethany. The whole spiritual realm stands still in anticipation, saints awaiting victorious triumph while the forces of darkness tremble in fear of the total defeat that death itself will soon suffer not far from Lazarus's grave, on Calvary.

Jesus does not walk into the grave. He does not step into death's domain. He stands outside and commands the dead to come forth and walk into life. He calls out, "Lazarus, come forth!" (John 11:43 NKJV).

> Jesus does not walk into the grave. He does not step into death's domain. He stands outside and commands the dead to come forth and walk into life.

And Lazarus walks out! Suddenly the cries of mourners together with the sobs of the sisters stop and turn into a jubilant cry of victory! Faith displaces fear, just as fear drowns out faith! And Martha sees the glory of God as Jesus has promised.

* * *

The earthly ministry of Jesus was about to end. From Bethany He went up to the Holy City. He returned to Jerusalem triumphant—riding on a donkey and fulfilling the prophecy (Zechariah 9:9; Luke 19:28–40). People greeted Him as king, covering the road with palm branches and stretching their robes over the pavement. But Jesus was fully aware that the same crowd that was shouting *Hosanna!* would be shouting *Crucify Him!* in just a few days.

Before His ascension, the resurrected Christ came back to Jerusalem and led His disciples to Bethany, where He blessed them, entrusting them with the Great Commission. From there He ascended up into the heavens (Luke 24:50). Perhaps Lazarus, Mary, and Martha were standing right there as witnesses having accepted this command from the Lord Himself.

Your faith has saved you. Believe and fear not!

Mary and Martha, having seen and experienced so much in their own lives, fearlessly went on to fulfill the Lord's Great Commission. Nothing can be greater than seeing God's glory made manifest in your life together with those who have found Jesus by believing on Him.

Fear not, just believe!

• LIFE LESSONS •

ABOUT GOD. "The Lord is close to the brokenhearted and saves those who are crushed in spirit" (Psalm 34:18). Bethany was a small town that only had sick and poor people inhabiting it, but Jesus loved to visit there. **"So do not fear, for I am with you; do not be dismayed, for I am your God. I will strengthen you and help you; I will uphold you with my righteous right hand" (Isaiah 41:10).**

ABOUT US. Do not worry and do not fret does not mean we should sit idly by. Jesus drew attention to Martha's approach and attitude instead. There is a difference between eternal and trivial things. Often we overestimate the importance of temporary, material things. Yet if we were to venture just five or ten years into the future, how many of them would truly matter? We make choices by prioritizing. So, do not worry about many things; instead, choose that which is eternal and cannot be taken away from you. Choose to invest yourself, your time, and strength into the things that will last forever. People and relationships are immeasurably more important than to-do lists, events, and projects. **"But seek first the kingdom of God and His righteousness, and all this shall be added unto you" (Matthew 6:33 NKJV).**

ABOUT LIFE. Everyone has their own journey. Honestly, universal norms and standards of acceptable good behavior don't really exist, but we have somewhat exaggerated criteria by which most people divide everyone into categories: good and bad, successful and unlucky, the righteous and the sinful. But God says in His Word, **"There is none righteous no not one ...all have sinned and**

fall short of the glory of God" (Romans 3:10, 23 NKJV). Even the righteous brother of the prodigal son was not righteous enough because he was prideful and the Pharisees who looked down on sinful tax collectors were themselves made blind by self-righteousness. We all need Jesus. So, instead of saying Lord, tell her, it is better to say, **"Test me, O Lord, and see if there be any wicked way in me" (Psalm 139:24).**

ABOUT FEAR. I think absolutely every person has experienced fear in some way—and not necessarily physically. Humanity has an enemy who seeks to destroy our souls. He wields fear as a dangerous weapon against men, women, and children. One seed of fear is enough; having been sown, it will grow and expand, displacing everything else, paralyzing and choking its victims like a boa constrictor firmly tightening its grip. There's only one antidote to fear: faith. The two cannot coexist. We tend to believe those whom we love and who love us in return. Faith in God abides in His love and acceptance. **"There is no fear in love. But perfect love drives out fear, because fear has to do with punishment. The one who fears is not made perfect in love" (1 John 4:18).**

ABOUT THE "STENCH" OF THE "DEAD" AMONG US. Don't rush to judgment, writing off situations or people as hopeless and "dead." We can infinitely trust the Lord because our God not only heals but resurrects the dead! How badly do we want to see our own supernatural victory? There's only one way this can happen—by turning off our fears and turning on our faith, because Jesus Himself told us to believe **"and you shall see the glory of God!" (John 11:40).** "As **surely as I live, declares the Sovereign Lord, I take no pleasure in the death of the wicked, but rather that they turn from their ways and live" (Ezekiel 33:11).** Love is patient.

OKSANA.
NEW MARRIAGE—
SAME HUSBAND

The small wedding became one of the brightest moments in my life. Young, tall, and beautiful, a couple stood in a tiny hall of our church against a backdrop decorated with branches and fresh flowers. The unveiled bride wore a plain dress and held a small bouquet in her pale hands. This bouquet was made with much love by her good friend, who is one of a handful of guests witnessing this marriage. It was a typical weekday, but this was no ordinary event. Beside the couple stood an eight-year-old boy, their son.

Oksana is getting married for the second time—but to the same man whom she married ten years ago. They married and divorced. The man is still the same, yet he is completely different. This wedding is a day of victory, a victory won in an epic battle in which there are no geographical, political, or national borders. This war rages on at every moment every day, affecting people of different ages, cultures, and social status by destroying our most sacred bonds, the family.

All this conflict began back in the Garden of Eden when God created man. I am talking about the creation of mankind, except not in its usual sense but rather as God had originally intended. "So God created mankind in his own image, in the image of God he created them; male and female he created them" (Genesis 1:27). It turns out that the perfect man God made, a man in his fullness, was not singular but plural: He created man... He created them.

Nevertheless, even there in the very beginning amid the most ideal setting, the enemy was already present, a serpent whose sabotage began with a single seed of doubt sown in the heart of Eve sprouting distrust. *You deserve more*, he whispered. *Life would be so much better. You are being fooled; you don't really have to obey. Why would anyone limit your freedom?*

That was the serpent's handwriting, and ever since then he continues to whisper into the willing ears of unsuspecting daughters of Eve. And countless Adams still hear *the husband shall rule over his wife* (Genesis 3:16) much louder than "Husbands, love your wives, just as Christ loved the church and gave himself up for her" (Ephesians 5:25), resulting in families falling apart.

Men and women seldom divorce for good reasons. Usually relationships fail because things just snowball; small trivial demands, misunderstandings, unforgiveness, and unwillingness to put each other first accumulate until they bury love like an avalanche, causing it to grow cold.

> Usually relationships fail because things just snowball; small trivial demands, misunderstandings, unforgiveness, and unwillingness to put each other first accumulate until they bury love like an avalanche, causing it to grow cold.

If we look closer, families break up because they don't have spiritual glue. This happens when the couple remove from the center of the family the One Who can glue them together, Who can hold them safe and secure in His hands. Marital glue consists of love. God *is* love. Therefore, when it comes to marriage, God is our Super Glue—His presence unites us inseparably.

Oksana met her future husband when both of them were in high school; he was sixteen, she was fifteen. She was bright and spirited, a tall and slender brunette with big brown eyes. He was calm and good natured and a little shy, a natural blond with piercing blue eyes. They both came from large families, his from Ukraine and hers from Russia. As immigrants in America, the Slavic kids keep together at school, they become friends, and sometimes friendships blossom into love.

At first, Oleg would carry her heavy textbooks during recess and from class to class; then he started driving her home in his car. He was already working in a body shop, and, as it turned out, Oleg was not only kindhearted and generous but also had skillful hands. Young people in Washington can get their driver's license when they turn sixteen, but car insurance is very expensive for most teens. So high schoolers continue to ride the bus, with the exception of those who manage to earn money for gas and insurance. Those get to drive their own cars to school. In any case, the first car of a typical American teenager is nothing to brag about, but everyone's heads turned when Oksana, a beauty, drove onto that schools parking lot in her bright red BMW convertible—and truth be told, Oleg was the sole reason behind it. Because he really cared what kind of car his girl was driving, he helped Oksana buy a slightly damaged vehicle and repaired it with his own hands, proving his love for her in this way. And of course, they celebrated their graduation together.

So in love and so young, they were eager to turn the page, leaving the school years behind and stepping into adulthood. Together.

Well, if they love each other, let them marry! Both of their families agreed. *They are so young and so in love! Look at them, a match made in heaven—the perfect couple!*

Soon came the huge wedding with a couple hundred guests attending the ceremony. They were blessed by the pastor, and everyone wished them joy and true happiness. Months of preparation and planning every detail beginning with the first photo shoot for their invitations, the guest list and dinner menu, the wedding decor and the flower arrangements, the wedding photographer and videographer, the wedding dress and limo ride, dressing the whole wedding party, the DJ, and final plans for their honeymoon—so much preparation has gone into this long-awaited wedding that only lasted for a few hours: the birth of their new family when the two become one.

For couples, the wedding day is like the proverbial alarm clock. It awakens the lovers from the state of euphoria when we idealize each other to the reality of normal life. We finally get to meet the real person we fell in love with, their true self without any makeup or pretense. This is where the rubber meets the road, and although we can deal with our own shortcomings and cultural misgivings, the same cannot be said about sudden and dangerous maneuvers when the marriage boat begins to sway as it crashes onto shore. Merging two paths into one can lead to nowhere.

Only a few months have passed since the wedding, but this young bride is spending her evenings alone already. Her husband comes from work to eat a home-cooked meal and then leaves to spend the rest of the evening with his friends. When he finally returns, he is drunk. Seeing this, she mostly cries, with periodic squabbles and mutual accusations in between. *Can a marriage survive when love is present, but the harmony is gone? Maybe this is not love.*

Both of them want to have children, and having become pregnant, Oksana hopes that with the new baby, her husband will spend more time at home and less with his friends. A child can also be a kind of glue that keeps a family together because it introduces both parents to a completely different kind of love. This connection is so strong that if someone attempts to divide this union, the separation is never benign, always tearing a chunk of flesh, leaving behind a bloody wound that can never heal.

But there also exists a spiritual darkness that creeps in through drugs and alcohol, devouring the souls of sons and daughters, mothers and fathers indiscriminately, and leaving a path of destruction in its wake. When their baby boy was just two years old, Oksana learned that Oleg had started taking drugs on top of his drinking habit. It was a terrible blow.

> *What should I do now?*
> *Where can I run?*
> *Is there any help for me?*

Her husband understood his own predicament, and he assured her of his love and faithfulness. He promised to quit, but he just couldn't do it. Yet, she believed him. He kept promising to quit, and he really wanted to, but he simply couldn't cope.

The next few years were the hardest. He would make attempts to better his life. Short periods of happiness were followed by confusion and scandals. Then forgiveness, new promises, and broken promises. They sought spiritual guidance from pastors and ministers, and with hearts full of hope, they prayed. Time passed, the boy grew, but hope of making any progress vanished.

> Short periods of happiness were followed by confusion and scandals. Then forgiveness, new promises, and broken promises.

Then they divorced.

Oksana and her son were now alone. She got herself a job plus a second part time job on top. When her boy turned five, he started school. Days went by quickly, but nights would drag on ever so lonely, tormenting her with endless questions: *What will happen to us? How will we live? What kind of man will my boy grow up to be? He needs a father, a role model, and I need a husband.*

"What God has joined together, let no man separate" (Matthew 19:6). Those words were not addressed to any third party or an outside force trying to invade the sacred union of the couple. Instead, at the end of the wedding ceremony, these words are spoken directly to the newlyweds themselves, instructing the two not to split apart their own family unit. Honestly, when marriage falls apart, people seldom take personal responsibility for the breakup; usually they blame each other. Sometimes even a third party gets the blame: it was because of alcohol or drugs or laziness and financial problems. Or it was infertility or "we are no longer in love." The union once so tightly bound by love "begins to fall apart," as if everything that happens to us is arbitrary, without us having any say or any personal responsibility for it.

Oleg periodically reappeared. He continued to care for his wife and son and asked her for a second chance in hopes that they could put their family back together. But he couldn't keep his promises, and he slipped back into his drunken state. Oksana couldn't believe him any longer. When trust is broken, relationship ceases to exist.

Then came the New Year, a family holiday. But if there is nobody to share it with, it is no longer a holiday. Most of us summarize last year, making resolutions and plans for the future on the eve of the New Year. Oksana's friend invited her to celebrate this New Year with a small new church—a good opportunity to meet new people.

> Oksana's trusting heart was badly wounded, and it seemed she could no longer believe anyone. But her healing was made possible by Jesus Himself.

This invitation became her turning point, healing Oksana's heart and her whole family. Her trusting heart was badly wounded, and it seemed she could no longer believe anyone. But her healing was made possible by Jesus Himself, Who was waiting for her inside this church among her new friends. Yes, she always knew about Jesus, but this time

He wanted to take her on a new journey of healing through the power of forgiveness.

Oksana began to attend this new church with her son. Oleg would pick his son up for the weekends, and they arranged to meet at church. One time he arrived a little earlier and entered the hall during service. Then it happened again. And another time.

Previously, Oksana had thought that it was only Oleg who needed to change. *After all, he needs to get rid of addiction, he must earn my trust again, and he needs to prove that he is changed and that everything can be different.*

Yes, she prayed for their family, for Oleg, but the more she prayed, the more she heard herself asking God to work on her own heart and attitude.

And this miracle began inside her own heart first. Everything that took place afterward was like a chain reaction: heart enlightened, forgiveness, hope, and love.

> The more she prayed, the more she heard herself asking God to work on her own heart and attitude. And this miracle began inside her own heart first.

The more she prayed, the more Oleg would reappear. He made new promises, like a dozen times before, only now he kept them.

How long can this last? She thought, *As soon as he gets his way, he will be back at it. We've been divorced for four years now. Should I make the same mistake twice?* Yes, she was doubtful.

Several times and without warning, Oksana came to Oleg's place of work, and together they went to take a random drug test. He was clean. He was keeping it together because he finally realized that holding onto the hand of his heavenly Father would keep him in line on the straight and narrow path.

One Sunday, when the three of them were together at church, Oleg came forward and knelt at the altar. In the presence of his wife, son, and the whole church, he acknowledged that needed help. It seems that it was then he stretched out his hand and put it into the hand of his heavenly Father wholeheartedly and forever. This was the only way he could lead his family. Oleg received forgiveness from God, and with it he also received forgiveness from his family.

By turning to God, we receive access to the throne of grace, where we can find strength and divine help. His redemption happened miraculously, without any time in rehab or twelve-step programs. When Oleg's heart opened to Jesus, He filled it with His love. Oleg's soul became so full there simply was no room left for any addiction. Oleg became a servant of Christ, and in that moment, he gained his true freedom.

> By turning to God, we receive access to the throne of grace, where we can find strength and divine help.

We can only impart that which we have received ourselves. Second chances can't be given by those who proudly beat their drum reveling in their own self-righteousness. Only those who have been to the cross, who have placed this cross at the very center of their lives as an example of the forgiveness that they themselves have received, can extend this gift to others. They simply cannot *not* forgive.

It is a Sunday and a sunny day. I stand in the hallway meeting the members of our church and greeting guests before service. Some of them I see for the first time as I stretch out my hand and say hello, inviting them to come inside the sanctuary. Others are regular church members, our friends who through the years have become our second family.

As I look through the glass doors, I see a beautiful family coming up the steps—young parents and a teenage boy walking next to them. The father is holding a girl, the little green-eyed blonde bouncing in his arms; the mother is cradling her pregnant belly. They are expecting their third child, another princess.

Their teenage son is already part of our ministry team in the church. He serves in our media department operating a video camera, making it possible for services to be available online. His dad is teaching middle schoolers in our Sunday school, is a Bible school student, and never misses the opportunity to tell someone about Jesus, be it in a coffee shop or on the street corner and even to his clients at work. Today, Oksana is a happy wife and mother; she looks at her men with love and gratitude, cheering them on in everything they do.

I do not know how often she goes down memory lane remembering those lonely nights she spent with her young boy, worrying about the future laying waste to the best years of her youth. I bet she doesn't do it much. Now she has a beautiful new home, welcoming guests and friends where she and her husband lead a small group. Every day Oksana's husband comes from work to a home-cooked meal (everyone who has tried Oksana's cooking loves it, and those who haven't can admire her skills following her Instagram stories).

Today as people look at their family, they will have a hard time believing that everything you just read above is about them, about our Oleg and Oksana.

And if in passing we suddenly remind them of their past, they always say that only God could have accomplished this kind of radical transformation in them.

When God is at the center of our life, given first place within our family, everything else falls into its proper place. Life becomes meaningful and filled with eternal purpose. It is precisely through these eternal values that we can experience life in full living color. We are together because we are glued together by this "Super Glue"—not the Hollywood kind of love whose meaning is perverted by this world but glued by true love—Love with a capital L. This Love that gave us hope and second chance teaches us to do the same for others.

• LIFE LESSONS •

ABOUT GOD. Our God is a God of second chances, long-suffering, all-merciful, and forgiving. On the pages of the Bible, we read stories of people who were like us—making mistakes, repenting, and getting a second chance from God. The prophet Jonah got his second chance and went on to preach to the hated Ninevites; the judge of Israel Samson, having first failed and suffered defeat, asked God for a chance and avenged the defeated Israelites by destroying the wicked Philistines; David, Saul, the apostle Peter, and the prodigal son—all of them and many others were granted a second chance. God is Love. Love gives second chances and does not remember the past. **"Their sins and lawless acts I will remember no more" (Hebrews 10:17).**

ABOUT US. By giving man freedom, God gave him the capacity for change—both for the good and for the bad. Those who are successful and prosperous today can become poor and miserable tomorrow and vice versa. **"So, if you think you are standing firm, be careful that you don't fall!" (1 Corinthians 10:12).** Where a person stands now is the result of his past choices, and accordingly, where we are headed tomorrow is largely determined by steps taken today. Whatever may be your situation today, you are never doomed. For those who know God there is always hope and a way out of any situation. No, there is no magic wand. In many respects hard work and effort to overcome yourself are of utmost importance, but change is possible! **"But grow in the grace and knowledge of our Lord and Savior Jesus Christ" (2 Peter 3:18).**

ABOUT LIFE. A lot of life is built on trust. When we are deceived or betrayed, trust is broken, lost, and gone. Trust cannot be restored. You cannot glue the old, shattered pieces back together again. You will need a new one, a new decision to believe again. Trust is not always earned or deserved, but it can be given as credit in advance. And this gracious credit of trust is what inspires us to strive for change. **"Accept one another, then, just as Christ accepted you, in order to bring praise to God" (Romans 15:7).**

ABOUT SECOND CHANCES. Starting with Adam and Eve, absolutely every human on this planet has experienced failure; if they didn't fail utterly, at least they stumbled. "Is anyone without sin?" This question is rhetorical for sure. Those who refuse to offer a second chance undoubtedly have no idea how much they themselves have been forgiven. **"A person's wisdom yields patience; it is to one's glory to overlook an offense" (Proverbs 19:11).**

ABOUT FAMILY. An ideal family with an ideal relationship is purely a figment of our imagination. In real life, perfect families don't exist. While we are still humans living on this planet, we struggle between that which we must do and our own selfish desires; the war of flesh against the spirit continues. Families that manage to stay together have long decided to choose love over trivial small victories in the epic battle between two imperfect beings. **"But be kind and compassionate to one another, forgiving each other, just as in Christ God forgave you" (Ephesians 4:32).**

FIVE DAUGHTERS OF ZELOPHEHAD. A CASE FOR SOCIAL JUSTICE

My parents are very wealthy people, mostly because of my mother—it was she who made my father a very rich man by giving him three sons and five daughters. *I live in a flower garden*, my father would always say. I remember when I was a teenager, he would call us by saying, "My dearest daughters, Zelophehad's daughters." None of us had any idea what it actually meant. I thought that it must have been a figure of speech, or maybe he was comparing us to some distant relative, Zelophehad, who also must have had five daughters.

A few years later, when I began to show interest in reading the Bible for myself and read beyond the New Testament, Psalms, and the Book of Proverbs, I came across a story about the daughters of Zelophehad. It was a very short story that seemed unremarkable. Twenty years later I was reading through the Bible once again, and while reading the Book of Numbers, I stopped and pondered their story.

Suddenly, the five daughters of Zelophehad unfolded in front of me in full living color. The five sisters are mentioned in three different books of the Bible: Numbers, Joshua, and Chronicles. Four times the Scripture lists them all by name, but it only mentions one episode from their lives: a legal case uniting all five unmarried girls. They had one unifying goal in mind and would overcome many obstacles to reach it.

> **The daughters of Zelophehad son of Hepher, the son of Gilead, the son of Makir, the son of Manasseh, belonged to the clans of Manasseh son of Joseph. The names of the daughters were Mahlah, Noah, Hoglah, Milkah and Tirzah. They came forward and stood before Moses, Eleazar the priest, the leaders and the whole assembly at the entrance to the tent of meeting and said, "Our father died in the wilderness. He was not among Korah's followers, who banded together against the Lord, but he died for his own sin and left no sons. Why should our father's name disappear from his clan because he had no son? Give us property among our father's relatives."**

> So Moses brought their case before the Lord, and the Lord said to him, "What Zelophehad's daughters are saying is right. You must certainly give them property as an inheritance among their father's relatives and give their father's inheritance to them.
>
> "Say to the Israelites, 'If a man dies and leaves no son, give his inheritance to his daughter. If he has no daughter, give his inheritance to his brothers. If he has no brothers, give his inheritance to his father's brothers. If his father had no brothers, give his inheritance to the nearest relative in his clan, that he may possess it. This is to have the force of law for the Israelites, as the Lord commanded Moses.'" (Numbers 27:1–11)

Millions of Jews wandered in the desert, walking in circles for forty long years. Like a dramatic motion picture, the story of their exodus tells of blood curdling generational slavery and countless deaths, of unbearable suffering followed by a strange collective madness as they grumbled and complained in the heat of the desert, craving garlic and the sight of the pyramids while wishing to go back under the whips of their Egyptian slave masters. Now the wilderness silently lay behind them; it would forever keep their fathers bones, scattered by the millions throughout its desert landscape.

> They Jews stood looking at the land flowing with milk and honey, and a renewed sense of hope stirred within them.

The price for their father's rebellion had been paid in full by the very people who dared to murmur on their journey of great exodus. God's verdict was harsh. Every man and woman whose feet walked on the bottom of the Red Sea would perish in the wilderness. Even those who had survived the snake bites; all who survived the heat, thirst, and hunger; all who dreamed of this earthly paradise, the promised land—in the end, none of them would ever enter it. All would die, except for two: Joshua and Caleb. But all their children would enter the land as promised, millions of young people who didn't remember the snakes nor the Red Sea and had only heard stories about Egypt. Those who have buried their disobedient parents in the wilderness behind them would walk into this land.

And forty years after the exodus, they stood at the borders of their earthly paradise. Before they could enter, the land was divided between their tribes and clans, giving them legal possession of cities and territories they still had to conquer. The Twelve Tribes were given their land by casting lots, as the Lord had commanded them. This way everyone had a fair chance at owning the land. Later they would pass this inheritance to the next generation within their tribes, keeping it in the family forever by giving it the names of their fathers, thus keeping their memories alive. They renamed the conquered cities and villages after their forefathers this way. Many of the landmarks as well would bear a Hebrew name. But somehow, despite this well-thought-out system, not everyone had their fair chance at ownership, and one such case was brought before Moses.

Five young women: Mahlah Noah, Hoglah, Milkah, and Tirzah.

Five young women without a father or husbands to fight on their behalf.

Five women in Middle Eastern culture 3,500 years ago.

Five women living in a refugee camp, a tent city with at least two million other people, decided to seek an audience with Moses himself.

Some may think that one day the girls went to fetch water and Moses just happened to be standing there right there by the well, so they jumped at the opportunity, and smiling ever so sweetly, asked him for a favor. Right? No, it was not that easy.

Because of Jethro, Moses's father-in-law who witnessed the endless lines of plaintiffs, day and night, presenting their cases before Moses, a better system of justice had been established in Israeli society. First, the plaintiff would petition his request to the foreman or a village judge. If he found the question too difficult to resolve, he would direct the plaintiff higher up, to one of the judges overseeing fifty divisions. The higher up would be more knowledgeable but their schedule much busier, so the line to get to them would be much longer as well. Then came the judge overseeing 100, then over 1,000, then the chief justice over 10,000, and finally the "supreme court justice" overseeing 100,000 people.

Moses alone could not deal with more than two million people all by himself. In addition, he preferred spending time in the presence of his best friend, the Holy God of Israel. Sometimes he would spend forty days on the mountain top; other times he spent countless hours in the tabernacle, a place of God's presence. Moses was unlike any other man; he was holy. His holiness permeated his face, with the divine light shining so bright that simply looking at him was painful for mere mortals. Now, could anyone just come and make an appointment to see him? Of course not. No one could disturb the holy man for mere trivialities.

I imagine Moses as a wise, old, bearded man surrounded by a group of noblemen. As he began to listen to the young women's request, his eyes grew wider and wider in surprise. All five of them came with the very short same question, an idea that no one had voiced before, and he must have wondered if they were genuine or delusional. On top of that, their family's reputation was not the best one can hope for. But they seemed very convincing, and they didn't look like they would take no for an answer.

> I imagine Moses as a wise, old, bearded man surrounded by a group of noblemen. As he began to listen to the young women's request, his eyes grew wider and wider in surprise.

We can only imagine how many obstacles these young sisters had to overcome, knowing a little bit of history and culture of that time; how many "your honors" they had to convince of the importance of their case. Their brief story on the pages of Scripture only tells us that they had an audience with Moses.

In the context of that time, everyone still remembered how a conversation with Moses could end if someone was insistently bent on pushing their own version of the truth. One such plaintiff who had brazenly demanded his own version of truth and justice had been cast down into hell right in the middle of his own court appearance, to the horror of everyone around him. The young daughters of Zelophehad knew this story too well; the rebellion of the revolutionaries Korah, Dathan, and Abiram against Moses was the talk of the town. And they knew exactly how not to ask for justice.

Standing before Moses and the priest Eleazar, among the noblemen and all the people, these young women had a keen sense of understanding the difference between seeking new ways and rebelling against God-given authority. So they began their short petition by talking about their father, making the point that they do not ask this for themselves, but for their deceased father's memory. It was about preserving his name among his people. I believe that this might have been the real reason why they got a positive resolution in their case. By emphasizing "our father did not participate in Korah's rebellion against Moses," they say he took no part in it. Why did the sisters find it necessary to communicate this detail? So what if he did or not? But they came with this as if to say, *We are not rebels either.* Their motivation was not to bring disagreement and complaints, rather, they had a legitimate request.

The Jewish oral tradition tells us that Zelophehad was the old man who collected firewood on that Sabbath when God struck him dead, thus making his death a vivid illustration to the fourth commandment, "Remember the Sabbath day, to keep it holy." But he could have died for another sin. Didn't they all die in the desert for the sin of grumbling against God? Perhaps he was just one of the many thousands who were sick of eating manna under the desert heat. But even those who sinned and died "for their own sins" could have hope that their children and grandchildren would inherit the promised land. Yes, all could have this hope except those like Zelophehad, for without a son, his lineage and inheritance ceased to exist.

We are not asking for ourselves, the young women implied as they pleaded, "Why should the name of our father disappear?" And Moses heard the familiar sound of a cry from the heart of an intercessor. He himself knew this cry too well because he was the constant intercessor for his people. Yet their request seemed too bold and specific: "give us a possession among our father's brothers" (Numbers 27:4 NASB). The five young women—Mahlah, Noah, Hoglah, Milkah, and Tirzah—were united by this single goal: preserving their father's inheritance.

> Moses heard the familiar sound of a cry from the heart of an intercessor. He himself knew this cry too well because he was the constant intercessor for his people.

But they did not come to accuse Moses of bias or misogyny and patriarchy.

They were not about to start a revolution shouting about injustice. Their motive was solid and they stood on solid ground; therefore, the earth beneath them did not swallow them up. Nor did Moses dismiss their case; he did not send the sisters home to humble themselves while they cooked and cleaned in hopes that someday someone with land rights would come and marry them.

He actually took them seriously, searching through the laws and regulations he had received from the Lord. And finding no such provision in the law, he went to ask God personally. *What! Moses, are you serious? There are millions of people here; time is very short; we have bigger problems. And you would bother God to ask about these girls?* Yes! Because God also took them seriously.

And God Himself answered.

> **What Zelophehad's daughters are saying is right. You must certainly give them property as an inheritance among their father's relatives and give their father's inheritance to them.**
>
> **Say to the Israelites, "If a man dies and leaves no son, give his inheritance to his daughter."** (Numbers 27:7–8)

Thus was added the first amendment to God's law, and everyone would reap its benefit for years to come. Later on, King David would write about it like this: "[The Lord] delights in every

> Turns out that it is possible to find new ways without rebelling against God-given authority. The birth of something new must not always lead to the death of the old.

detail of their lives" (Psalm 37:23 NLT). Turns out that it is possible to find new ways without rebelling against God-given authority. The birth of something new must not always lead to the death of the old.

Wealth and ownership obliges its owner to stewardship. But this short story about the sisters has one more important detail we must not overlook. These young women were honorable and virtuous.

They lived righteous lives before their God, observing all His commandments, because they valued justice. Thus, the girls were ready to meet any preconditions in their quest for justice, so they married the men who were chosen for them—their own cousins from their own tribe.

"So Zelophehad's daughters did as the Lord commanded Moses. Zelophehad's daughters—Mahlah, Tirzah, Hoglah, Milkah, and Noah—married their cousins on their father's side. They married within the clans of the descendants of Manasseh son of Joseph, and their inheritance remained in their father's tribe and clan" (Numbers 36:10–12).

These girls were brave, but they were not indignant, daring, or rude. They came to Moses with humility and received their inheritance, taking full responsibility for it, subjecting their personal lives to the same goal of justice and honor.

What is an inheritance? Gold crowns and royal titles, lavish estates and family jewels? Not necessarily. Those are things from the movies and fairy tales; they have nothing whatsoever to do with real life for most of us. Nevertheless, we all long for something grander, something truly meaningful. Deep on the inside we all thirst for virtue, honor, and nobility. We hang on to our own heritage, keeping the thin thread of generational lineage in our memories, keeping the names of our forefathers sacred.

> Deep on the inside we all thirst for virtue, honor, and nobility.

But this is not the only reason I find the story of the five sisters to be so profound. This account opens up a colorful illustration of the truth of our own spiritual inheritance as well as the rightful means of coming to possessing it. Everyone knows there is a right and the wrong way of taking something. There's God's way and there's man's way. And centuries later, these five young girls are still showing us the way how to ask and receive that which we are so desperately seeking today.

Think of it. A last will and testament becomes valid only after the death of its testator, the person writing the will. You and I have been made beneficiaries of the last will and testament of our Lord Jesus Christ by God our Father, Who has provided for this inheritance: He has granted us His salvation, peace, love, purpose, and dignity upon His Son's death. No one can earn or purchase His inheritance; it is given freely, but can only be attained by righteous means. Those who come to possess it can pass it on to the next generation. He who has full possession of this divine inheritance has the right to pass it on to his children and his children's children. For one can only give that which one truly owns.

We all had earthly parents. What have we inherited from our parents? The color of our eyes, the shape of our noses, our genes? Yes, all that, and many attribute their success in life to their parents as well. But our heavenly Father, Who has adopted us into His own family, gave us much more than that. He has provided the heavenly inheritance for His children, making us His heirs.

And these are the provisions of our inheritance:

• The Holy Spirit is the oath of our inheritance (Ephesians 1:13–14).

• God has blessed us with every kind of spiritual blessing in Christ (Ephesians 1:3–13).

• "Lord, you alone are my portion and my cup; you make my lot secure." (Psalm 16:5).

• We are the children of God, heirs of God, and joint heirs with Christ. God Himself has inscribed our names in His will (Romans 8:16–17).

• Salvation is our inheritance (Hebrews 1:14).

• God has opened our eyes so that we could see the wealth of the glorious inheritance He has prepared for His Saints (Ephesians 1:18).

• The gracious gift of life has been granted to us as women: daughters and wives and co-heirs with our husbands (1 Peter 3:7).

All these things have been freely given to every child of God—to all the sons and daughters of the Most High! Now, taking full possession of this divine inheritance, increasing it, and passing it on to our next generation becomes our relentless pursuit.

The Lord has made every provision for us even before we were born, but He has left the receiving and taking possession of our inheritance completely up to us. It is *up to us* whether or not we shall come into its full possession. It is *up to us* to set its attainment as our personal life's goal. It won't come easy. Even though it is freely given; nevertheless, it will take disciplined effort to see it come to fulfillment in our own lives, but striving for it is our God-given journey. To do so, we must overcome adversity, casting aside all fears together with any lingering doubt, becoming the embodiment of God's will here on this earth, and in so doing, we shall pass our inheritance to our own children's children. Because only those of us who will come to own it can leave this legacy for the generations to come.

> The Lord has made every provision for us even before we were born, but He has left the receiving and taking possession of our inheritance completely up to us.

We—the mothers, the daughters that birth the next generation—are in possession of the greatest of all earthly treasures: faith in God, His living Word, His wisdom, His presence and His unrelenting strength.

> We, in our own living rooms and kitchens, in our churches and communities, are the modern world changers!

We, all of us put together, taking possession of what God has promised to us right in the midst of the business of today's life, in our own living rooms and kitchens, in our churches and communities, are the modern world changers!

We shall carry the name of our Father to the ends of the earth advancing His kingdom because the wealth of our divine inheritance belongs to us and to our children and to all who will call on His Name.

And even though it will not be easy, though we will have hardships and deserts to walk through, obstacles and adversity to overcome, yet at the end of our journey, we will be looking back with a grateful heart, with a smile and a song in our hearts. "My share in life has been pleasant my part has been beautiful" (Psalm 16:6 NCV).

• LIFE LESSONS •

ABOUT GOD. Amendment to the law is possible. Ask God, because He has all the answers to any question that is not spelled out in the textbooks. Moses, having already received all the commandments and the law from the Lord, after hearing a new question that did not fit into his framework, went directly to the Lord and asked. And then he did as he was commanded. **"Where there is strife, there is pride, but wisdom is found in those who take advice" (Proverbs 13:10). "Call to me and I will answer you" (Jeremiah 33:3).**

ABOUT US. Check your motives. Sometimes not everything is to my liking. The daughters of Zelophehad were given their inheritance, but it came with one condition; they must marry within their own tribe. This drastically limited the choice of these bold and intelligent girls. But having passed their test for wisdom and decency, they had proved what God told Moses about them: They were right. Their motives were true and pure. They were not about to become revolutionaries seeking to overturn injustice by uncovering systemic bias and bigotry. The girls were completely focused on their goal—preserving their father's name—even when it limited their freedom. **"I the Lord search the heart and examine the mind, to reward each person according to their conduct, according to what their deeds deserve" (Jeremiah 17:10).**

ABOUT LIFE. My life is not just about me. Every one of us is part of something bigger: a family, a community, a nation. Are we willing to go the extra mile and not just for our own interests or benefits? Any public service limits and shifts the boundaries between our personal and common good. In the case of Zelophehad's daughters, the good—keeping their father's name alive, which introduced a new amendment to the law—also put a damper on their personal romantic lives. But, the girls would not relent **"not looking to your own interests but each of you to the interests of the others" (Philippians 2:4).**

ABOUT METHODS. Instead of revolution, choose evolution. Innovations should not be achieved by rebelling against existing order and leadership. There is a better way. Instead of being against people who were thoughtless or uncaring, it is better to be for a new and improved way of thinking. Make everything you touch flourish! **"They must turn from evil and do good; they must seek peace and pursue it. For the eyes of the Lord are on the righteous and his ears are attentive to their prayer, but the face of the Lord is against those who do evil" (1 Peter 3:11–12).**

ABOUT DETERMINATION. The courage of five young women changed the law. And to this day, every family in similar circumstance reaps the benefits of their achievement. This illustrates how today's decisions are changing not only our lives but are also making a difference for generations to come. **"For the Spirit God gave us does not make us timid, but gives us power, love and self-discipline" (2 Timothy 1:7).**

12

NAOMI.
THE JOY OF SECOND CHANCES

For ten years I had two mothers: my mom and his mom; my own mother and my mother-in-law (although I never called her that). Vasily and I married when we were twenty-six. Both of us were independent adults, having lived away from our parents for several years. But whatever the age of the newlyweds, whether very young or not so young, they are not only creating their new family, but also becoming a part of a larger family clan.

One's grand entrance into a larger family dynamic can be very different. Some are welcomed with open arms, making their transition positively natural; others are rejected offhand, forcing

> God uses our family as His tools for shaping and molding our character because these people will be connected to us for a lifetime.

a proceed-with-caution approach. Familial relationships play the biggest part in life. They can become the source of our greatest joy and the cause of our deepest pain. I always believed that nothing in my life is by coincidence. That is why I consider every single person in my path to be God-sent. This is especially true when it comes to our close relationships. God uses our family as His tools for shaping and molding our character because these people will be connected to us for a lifetime.

When I was born, my parents were in their twenties, but when my husband was born, his parents were in their forties. If you think of the age difference alone, their life experiences were closer to those of my grandparents than to my parents.

His mom had three sons; she never had an opportunity to raise a daughter and often spoke of it with regret. Life in Soviet culture was harsh, not affording any luxuries to women. That and being surrounded by four men had inadvertently shaped her outlook on life. She was strict and very plain. Not been spoiled by attention, she had aged while still young.

My mom, on the other hand, raised five daughters. She was both our best friend and our mom. When we were little, she spoiled us by braiding our hair and dressing us up in our Sunday best. Now we pick out her dresses and hairstyles to our liking.

I think every young bride realizes that she is gaining another older woman in her life, her husband's mother, with whom she will organize family dinners, parties, and holidays, interacting and consulting with her on everyday things, and maybe even going shopping together. But for such a relationship to be possible, one needs to go through welcoming and accepting each other, learning to understand and love one another.

Because we lived on the opposite sides of the planet, the first time I met my husband's mom was long after we were married. A typical sweet Russian babushka, she was kind and old with curly gray hair, which she always kept gathered in a lush bun covered by a thin translucent head scarf. I instantly felt that I was not what she had expected, but I could not tell what it was about me that throw her off. Could it be my bleached hair, or was it my jeans, but I definitely could tell that I did not match her perfect image of the proper daughter-in-law.

A few years later we moved from Russia closer to where my husband's parents lived, bringing our newborn daughter Katerina to America. Vasily and I were head over heels in love with our chubby-cheeked baby girl, but when we arrived and showed her off to his parents, his mother said, "Back in my village Kat'ka[5] was only good for a goat's name," and added that we should rename our daughter Christina. Christina sounded fine for someone else, but because our baby girl was already four months

---

[5] Kat'ka (pronounced with a soft K) is a short form of Katerina, often used in a derogatory manner.

old and already had a name—it was Katerina! After all, it was clearly written on her birth certificate and her passport.

The conflict was a bit bizarre. Two grown women and one little girl—one woman stubbornly refers to the baby as Christina, the other constantly and politely corrects her by saying, "Mom, our daughter's name is Katerina!" Nevertheless, we never clashed with his mom. We both tried to be polite, and we mostly talked about household things. My husband would constantly hug me right in front of his parents and without hesitating would say how much he loved me and how happy we were together. And if for some reason his mom expressed any disappointment, he would come and give her a big hug saying, "Don't worry, Mom, we love you. Everything will be fine."

A few years went by, and I didn't even notice when his mom stopped calling our Katerina Christina, when she stopped bringing those ugly, old-fashioned skirts for me to wear (she must have thought that I simply didn't have a long skirt to wear, and that is why I wear jeans). She stopped paying attention to my blond hair and whatever else she didn't like about me before. We now lived very close to them and would see them a few times per week.

We had a son and then another daughter, and I have absolutely no idea how would we have managed if it weren't for the help of my husband's parents. Of course, we tried to do it all by ourselves because Vasily's mother had diabetes, a bad heart, and high blood pressure, and they both were very old people. But they never once refused to come and watch our children. They sweetly called them the Russian way—Katerinochka, Pavlichyok, and Arianochka—and despite my protests, would always spoil the kids with gifts, sweets, and treats. All the walls of their apartment were covered by our photos and drawings and cards made by our children. They loved for us to come visit. Mom would cook her favorite dishes, and I would secretly persuade the children to try it and to give their grandma lots of praise.

She always called me sweet Olychka, and only now I understand that she would often invent the reasons for me to come and visit. In 2011, Mom died of a sudden heart attack. Just days before her death, she had asked me to come and translate the instructions on some new vitamin bottles. It was late in the evening. I had returned from our women's gathering at church and drove straight to her place. Back at home the children were already asleep, so I was not in any hurry. I remember how I started sharing with her what was on my heart, ministering to women, and I shared some of their stories with her. I shared things the Lord had shown to me and what I was sharing with the other women. And this seventy-one-year-old grandmother, who had never once believed that a woman can minister the Word of God, looked me in the eyes with tears and said, "Olychka, I always pray a blessing over you. May God give you much strength and wisdom." That night we never got to the bottles with vitamins. I walked out of their apartment, as always, carrying jars of homemade pickles (which we kept stacking on the shelf in our garage, unable to eat them all at once). I left holding a bag full of treats and with a deep sense of being loved.

A few month before her death, Vasily's mother had to have surgery. When we were at the hospital, I overheard one of her conversations. On that day the nurse who took care of her happened to be Russian-speaking, and when she came in to check on her, I went out of the room to make a phone call. The door was slightly open, and while I was searching in my phone, I overheard the nurse greet Mom. She asked her about the procedure and then about family. It was then that I heard Vasily's mother answer her question about me.

"A girl who was just in here? Oh, that was my sweet daughter." This was her deepest proclamation of love for me, and our love was mutual.

Remarkably, the Bible, which is a collection of sixty-six books, has two that are named after women. Their names were Ruth and Esther. Each book is about a woman, one woman was Jewish, but she became a wife of a pagan king; the other is the opposite—she was a pagan woman who married a Jewish man and became the grandmother to King David, taking her place in the lineage of our Savior Jesus Christ.

In literature, there is such a thing as the main character and a supporting character. The book is named after Ruth. She is at the center of the story and is considered the main character. But to me it seems as if this book is about Naomi. It tells the whole story of her life and her family's struggle to survive. We get to witness her transformation from a happy woman into a bitter widow who has buried both her sons; and then we see her turn back from Mara (which means *Bitter*) into a beautiful happy woman again, becoming a grandmother of Ovid. Midway, this drama turns into a romantic novel with a happy end.

Throughout history children, especially sons, were considered to be a blessing and a great wealth. But over the centuries of time, the importance and significance of a large family with relatives, heirs, and successors has lost its meaning. The values of parenthood are gradually being replaced by the search for self-realization, personal growth and development, career chasing, and just plain old comfort seeking. In Jewish culture, as in many others, childlessness was considered to be a grave curse as opposed to a blessing of having many children.

> *The values of parenthood are gradually being replaced by the search for self-realization, personal growth and development, career chasing, and just plain old comfort seeking.*

> **Children are an heritage of the Lord: and the fruit of the womb is his reward. As arrows are in the hand of a mighty man; so are children of the youth. Happy is the man that hath his quiver full of them: they shall not be ashamed, but they shall speak with the enemies in the gate. (Psalm 127:3–5)**

At one time, Elimelek was considered to be a successful and blessed man. He had a beautiful wife and two sons—he was a rich man, even though he did not possess any large plots of land in Bethlehem, nor was he of any nobility in his town.

But a day came for this father to decide what was more important for him, patriotism or taking care of his family. This question arose before Elimelek when their country was hit by severe famine. The time is about 1,000 years before Christ, one of the darkest periods in the history of the Kingdom of Judah. Wars died down, and the glorious exploits of Joshua, who had conquered the land for the Twelve Tribes of Israel, were long forgotten. Peace came, and it seemed that they should have thrived in this land of promise. After all, here where milk and honey flowed, they could happily raise their children and their flocks while worshiping their God, who gave them this life and freedom. But only a few had passed their faith in God to their descendants. Soon they forgot all about His commandments and decrees, wanting to be like the other nations, having statues for gods and idols to worship, and to do as they pleased in spite of what God had commanded them through Moses. This was the time when "Every man did that which was right in his own eyes" (Judges 21:25 KJV).

Time and time again, the people of Israel would backslide from God and, He would withhold His protection while trying to bring them back to Himself. Their enemies would rise up and attack them, they would suffer from famine and wars, and then God would send a deliverer, one of the judges, to rescue them.

Just like today, when trouble comes we all turn to God, and He, being our good God, always answers and saves us—for the second and third and fifth and tenth time. During one of these dark periods of falling away, Judea was struck by famine.

> When trouble comes we all turn to God, and He, being our good God, always answers and saves us—for the second and third and fifth and tenth time.

One can either overcome difficulties or try to avoid them, but it doesn't always work out. Sometimes, running away from one problem gets you into another. The difficulties have purpose; they are meant to shape us, change us, and refocus our perspective. Like a race with obstacles, no matter how hard it gets, you simply have to keep running, because turning onto the sidelines means you have forfeited your race. The whole purpose of the race is to cross the finish line having overcome all obstacles.

As Elimelek and Naomi stood in the middle of their barren field in Bethlehem, they hoped to make the right decision. Patriotism is great, but when our children's lives are at stake, then our will to protect them overshadows patriotism. So they fled from their homeland to the land of Moab to seek refuge on enemy territory as a rebellious teenager would run away from home, from the protection offered by his parents, because they had imposed limits on his freedom or disciplined him. They emigrated and, by doing so, demonstrated their distrust in God. Neither love for their country nor for their neighbors could keep them home when faced with impending starvation and death of their loved ones.

Who of us would cast the first stone at them when we have no idea what we would have done?

Unfortunately, they did not understand the words that Solomon would later write in his proverbs: "My son, do not despise the Lord's discipline, and do not resent his rebuke" (Proverbs 3:11).

The Moabites were the wicked nation descending from Lot, who had a son by his eldest daughter. This story may be the most shocking perversion in all of the Old Testament. Lot had left the city of Ur of the Chaldeans with his uncle Abraham, but he did not share his faith or destiny. He moved his family into Sodom and Gomorrah. Then came the judgment day. God shared with His friend Abraham, how He intended to destroy these cities ravaged with sin.

Abraham begged God to spare his nephew's family and would not relent. And so the angels, messengers of God, brought Lot out of Sodom giving him strict orders: "Run for your lives! And don't look back" (Genesis 19:17 NLT). But Lot's wife did not heed their warning. She turned and looked back; thus, she was left standing halfway between life and death as a pillar of salt and as a reminder to us all.

Lot's two daughters then decided to take the initiative of continuing their father's lineage by having his children. Each daughter slept with her own father and gave birth to a son, from whom entire nations came about, the Ammonites and the Moabites.

Centuries later, the descendants of Abraham would come to take possession of the land on which these nations had settled— and they would be enemies forever. Nevertheless, this is where Elimelek took his family to seek refuge from the famine, away from his God-given land. They came and settled in Moab. We do not know exactly what happened, but the father, the head of the household, died, leaving his wife and two sons to fend for themselves in this foreign land.

It is interesting to explore the meaning behind the names of these family members. Elimelek from Hebrew literally means *My God Is my King*; Naomi means *Delight*, but the names they gave to their sons are not as cheerful. Mahlon means *weakness*, or *illness*, and Chilion means *suffering*. What a difference in the names of the parents when compared to their children! Maybe the boys were weak or sick as infants, and Naomi was afraid to return with them to Judea, where famine raged on, but whatever the reason, they decided to settle and stay in Moab for good.

Moab was prosperous, its fields full of grain and its villages full of beautiful girls. Somehow they had forgotten that God did not allow the Jews to marry foreigners. The young men Mahlon and Chilion found brides for themselves and married. Naomi probably cheered up in hopes of having grandchildren. But ten years later, there were none.

Neither bride, Orpah nor Ruth, ever gave her any children. Instead of joy and long-awaited pregnancies, a double funeral befell them: both sons of Naomi died. Three deaths in one family left three grieving widows, a lot of tears and regret, and a lot of questions. Naomi, decided that her name Delight does not describe her any longer. She wanted her name to reflect her reality, so she renamed herself Mara, *Bitter*.

But suddenly, this hopeless darkness was cut through with a beam of gleaming light—good news from Judea. "Naomi heard in Moab that the Lord had come to the aid of his people by providing food for them" (Ruth 1:6).

Naomi's men have died. Their deaths were not her choice, but Naomi chose bitterness. Most often our circumstances are beyond our control, but who we become through these circumstances is completely up to us. God had visited His people, and this good news instilled faith and renewed hope in Naomi's heart. Long ago they chose to leave their homeland; now she must choose whether to return or stay. "Then she arose with her daughters-in-law that she might return from the land of Moab" (Ruth 1:6 NASB).

> Most often our circumstances are beyond our control, but who we become through these circumstances is completely up to us.

Three single women making a life-changing decision. All three were facing uncertainty, but they knew there would be different ramifications for the daughters-in-law. For Orpah and Ruth, it would be a crazy move to break away from their own families and culture, leaving behind their religion, and going toward the complete unknown. Even if they were very beautiful, in Judea, they would have three enormous setbacks: *Who would marry foreign-born widows with ten years of infertility?* Naomi understood this, and the farther they went from Moab, the more she doubted her decision.

Stop! This is about my life and my decision, she says, *and therefore, all future consequences are mine too.* This courageous old woman thanks her daughters-in-laws for their kindness toward her and her deceased sons. Then she tells them to go back home, insisting they stay in their homeland, to pursue their own happiness among their own people. They had been with her for ten long years, and she must have got used to them; she sure did love them, for true love is not self-seeking, so she wishes the best for them. Naomi blessed and hugged and kissed them and then continued on her journey.

She kept walking. But through the years of loving and caring for her son's wives, she had imparted into these girls the stories about Judea and the God of Israel, about the people of God and His faithfulness to them. And it had sprouted a seed in the heart of Ruth, making her heart turn away from her vile idols, the gods of Moab, toward Naomi and her God. Orpah returned home to her parents, but Ruth stayed, saying:

> **Where you go I will go, and where you stay I will stay. Your people will be my people and your God my God. Where you die I will die, and there I will be buried. May the Lord deal with me, be it**

ever so severely, if even death separates you and me. (Ruth 1:16–17)

These words would inflame the hearts of millions with passion as the most beautiful words of true love and loyalty—"till death do us part."

When the two women finally reached Bethlehem, they set the whole city in motion. People recognized the name but did not recognize the face of the sad and gray haired-woman Naomi had become. She thought that coming home and staying within the walls of her own house would heal her wounded heart, but on the contrary, it only made it bleed more, reminding her of her past happy life. What profound contrast in just ten years: she had a husband—now she was a widow; she had sons—now she was childless; she had prosperity—now she was empty handed; she had happiness—now she was suffering in deep despair! All that remained of her past was her name. But it no longer reflected her! Naomi had died with her husband and sons.

"Call me Mara!" she told her friends and neighbors, as if inner bitterness was not enough for her punishment, she wanted to hear it every time they spoke of her: Bitter, Bitterness.

Then suddenly everything turned, changing this drama into a romance. Naomi and Ruth came to Bethlehem just in time for the barley harvest. To provide food for herself and her mother-in-law, hardworking Ruth goes out into the fields to pick up fallen grain after the harvesters. By pure chance, it turned out that the very first field she entered belonged to

Naomi's relative Boaz, a noble man, a widower, who was both honorable and wealthy.

When Naomi heard of this, she told her daughter-in-law what she should do. After Ruth followed Naomi's advice, Boaz gathered the council of elders at the city's gate and he fulfilled his obligation to Ruth. According to the Law of Moses, the closest male relative must marry the childless widow of his brother to restore his brother's name.

> **Boaz announced to the elders and all the people, "Today you are witnesses that I have bought from Naomi all the property of Elimelek, Chilion, and Mahlon. I have also acquired Ruth the Moabite, Mahlon's widow, as my wife, in order to maintain the name of the dead with his property, so that his name will not disappear from among his family or from his hometown. Today you are witnesses!" (Ruth 4:9–10)**

So this pagan-born, previously childless Moabite, Ruth, received the greatest gift anyone can dream of on her wedding day. She became one of God's people. She received her blessing, the blessing that came not only from Naomi and Boaz, but from the One Whom she had chosen to worship—God Almighty. They blessed her to be like Leah and Rachel, which meant to have a blessed home and children. And just as she accepted Naomi's God and her people, she accepted this blessing—by faith. "Boaz took Ruth and she became his wife. When he made love to her, the Lord enabled her to conceive, and she gave birth to a son" (Ruth 4:13).

And whatever happened to Naomi? Her neighbors were just about to settle on her new name Mara when it simply evaporated, or rather, she was back to her old self, the happy Naomi. How can she be bitter when she is a grandmother holding the sweetest boy in her arms, a newborn baby, her long-awaited first grandson! Her transformation was so miraculous that seeing her made all her friends bless and glorify God. Naomi carried the baby in her arms, and the love for this child began to heal and restore her broken heart.

Looking at the now rejuvenated Naomi, her neighbors said, *Look*, "Naomi has a son!" (Ruth 4:17). The boy grew and became the father of Jesse, and one day he would become David's grandfather, becoming a chain in the lineage of Jesus Christ. How much of this would even be possible if Naomi had stayed back in Moab, succumbing to her depression and bitterness?

The Book of Ruth is a story that crushes all stereotypes about mother-in-law and daughter-in-law relationships. Where else would we meet a daughter-in-law who, according to the people around her, was "better . . . than seven sons" (Ruth 4:15)? It is a story of true devotion and love, a story of a good relationship and great reward for faithfulness. But above all, this is a story about God, Who gives second chances in the midst of hopelessness and suffering so that we can start everything anew again. The God Who gives beauty for ashes, restores the lost, and blesses all who turn to Him—even those who fell under the curse as did Lot's descendants.

• LIFE LESSONS •

ABOUT GOD. Our God is **"rich in mercy" (Ephesians 2:4).** The blessing is that every day we have a choice to make. Making the right choices today can redeem and restore the consequences of our previous wrong choice. We are granted grace that is new every morning. God speaks about the present: **"Because of the Lord's great love we are not consumed, for his compassions never fail. They are new every morning; great is your faithfulness" (Lamentations 3:22–23).**

ABOUT US. When faced with a problem, the first question we ask ourselves is What do I do? Analyzing the cause of our troubles will come later, because for now we are driven by a purely emotional response. Naomi made a move twice in her life; the first was a grave error, the second a decision that corrected that mistake. There is a difference between having an active position by taking responsibility for our actions and a reactive position by taking hasty steps in fear and mistrust. **"Give careful thought to the paths for your feet and be steadfast in all your ways" (Proverbs 4:26).**

ABOUT LIFE. Bad things happen to all people. Often we have no control over malevolence, but what our experience molds us into as we go through our suffering solely depends on us. Bitterness is a choice. Going through tragedy, some will heal, their wounds scarring over, while others never let themselves heal because they are constantly picking at their wounds.

Pain is a constant part of life; therefore, it is better to have rugged scars than infectious wounds hidden under a Band-Aid. We should not live in denial, hiding our pain, but we need to allow God to heal our heart and soul.

The Apostle James gives this advice: **Consider it pure joy, my brothers and sisters, whenever you face trials of many kinds, because you know that the testing of your faith produces perseverance. Let perseverance finish its work so that you may be mature and complete, not lacking anything. (James 1:2–4)**

ABOUT TROUBLES. Too often, by running away from our problems, we are attempting to run away from ourselves. Difficulties are like a treadmill; they are designed to help us overcome our weakness and to build up the muscles of our character, making sure that later on we can endure the burden of suffering.

No temptation has overtaken you except what is common to mankind. And God is faithful; he will not let you be tempted beyond what you can bear. But when you are tempted, he will also provide a way out so that you can endure it. (1 Corinthians 10:13)

ABOUT THE COST. An old proverb says, It was a blessing in disguise. Ruth had paid a heavy price by following her heart: she left her family and her people, overcame fear, and faced the unknown. This cost was an investment in her own future, and not for a moment did she regret it. Hindsight is twenty-twenty, they say. It is easy to rejoice looking at how well everything turned out. Yet it is immensely difficult to step into an unsettled future, into the unknown, even when you feel that it is the right step to take. Nevertheless, the Bible describes a virtuous woman like this: **"She is clothed with strength and dignity; she can laugh at the days to come" (Proverbs 31:25).**

13

GRANDMOTHER. FAITHFULNESS TO THE ENDS OF THE EARTH

I first visited Canada and the Americas Pacific Northwest at 23 years old, taking part in a Youth with a Mission conference. I am absolutely overwhelmed by the grandeur of the landscapes: the beauty of British Columbia, the splendor of Colorado, and, finally the magnificent Pacific Coast with its waterfalls and evergreen mountains. My first encounter with the Pacific Ocean is intense. I can scarcely keep my breath looking down on this indescribable beauty. The massive waves crash against sheer cliffs, and cold gusts of sudden wind mix with the roar of the ocean.

Just a short drive up the Oregon coast, I get to experience real sand dunes. My American friends take me up the slopes in an open jeep. Then we all have dinner in the small town of first, at a famous spot, Mo's Seafood and Chowder, and everyone has to try their signature dish—clam chowder in a bread bowl.

Life is so amazing! Just a few hundred miles away, right on the border with Oregon, lives a young man, Vasily Yarosh. He works here and heads a local Bible school in a town called Vancouver, Washington. It will only take a few years for us to meet in Kiev. We will marry and live in Moscow, where our first daughter, Katerina, will be born. Then, in another few more years, we will be living in America, right in these parts, where together with our three children, we will come to the ocean on weekends. We will walk here listening to the same roar and have dinner at that exact spot—Mo's restaurant—and my children will order that exact same dish—bread bowl with clam chowder. But all that will come later. For now, I just daydream while praying for my future family.

I am visiting here for just a few short weeks. I am sitting by an oversized window in my red, oversized, comfortable chair. I am bored, and I have tried every possible reclining position for the chair's backrest. Then I walk to a cafe to order myself a muffin with a cup of coffee. I go back up to the second floor and sit to drink my coffee in the same chair facing the window.

I am traveling from Oregon to Washington via Amtrak. The ride is so smooth that if it weren't for the rapidly changing landscapes in my window, I wouldn't believe that I am riding an actual train. In the absence of the usual *chugga-chugga, click-click*, the passenger car is not swaying from side to side, and I hear no sound of teaspoons rattling in the glass cups either. *How come this train is so quiet and smooth?* I wonder. Of course, I do not mind sitting by the window with a cup of coffee in my hand, passing through Salem, the capital of Oregon, and going down memory lane remembering other train rides from my childhood and youth, usually with a group of other Bible school students and mostly in cheap seats. And without me even noticing, my mind takes me way back to a time before my own very first train ride to the circus with my dad, to a time before I was even born. I begin to picture the story told by my father about his own very first and treacherous journey on a Siberian railroad.

* * *

A cold fall day in 1961. Novocherkassk railway station.

Novocherkassk is a small town near Rostov-on-Don, in southern Russia. A beautiful woman a little over 30 entered the train car. She walked in with great difficulty, clutching a large bundle close to her chest, but that was not all she carried; she was literally strung with small children and loads of baggage on all sides.

Does she have triplets? Or maybe two sets of triplets—three older boys and three little girls? When they all finally found seats and settled down on a bench next to their mother, you could start counting them and telling them apart; there were six of them. The boys who look like triplets were actually just one year apart: Peter, Paul, and Vladimir—ten, nine, and eight years old. And the girls, Lia, Lyuba, and Vera, were all two years apart— six, four, and two. The women sighed for a moment, untied her woolen shawl, straightened her sweaty hair, and carefully unwrapped the bundle, which she kept close to her heart the whole time. From the middle of the bundle came a faint cry. She had her newborn, Yakov, tightly swaddled in these blankets.

Where could this woman be traveling to with so many children? Where is her husband? This railcar, full of smoke and overfilled with people, was no place for little children; she should have bought tickets to the sleeping car instead, or at least to the passenger car where they would have had assigned setting. The passengers in the general car were mostly poor and vulgar people. No child should ever hear that kind of talk. The smoke and the sheer filth all around were not good for them for sure. By the end of the day, ev-

---

By the end of the day, everyone in the entire railcar knew that this woman was a Baptist, a member of a forbidden religious sect, and she was traveling with her children to join her husband, a minister, in Siberia, where he was sentenced to five years of hard labor in exile after his prison sentence.

---

eryone in the entire railcar knew that this woman was a Baptist, a member of a forbidden religious sect, and she was traveling with her children to join her husband, a minister, in Siberia, where he was sentenced to five years of hard labor in exile after his prison sentence.

It took seven days on the train to reach the city of Tomsk, with a layover in Novosibirsk, where everyone had to restamp their tickets.

Seven days with seven children.

I try to imagine a weeklong journey on the Trans-Siberian Railway with seven little kids almost sixty years ago. Today when we travel, I usually make myself a lists of things to take. This became a necessity, especially when our kids were younger. Obviously, back then, over half a century ago, the list could not have included disposable diapers, wet wipes, drinking water in plastic bottles, all kinds of little snacks and baby food. There would have been no bottle heaters, no backpacks for each child with their favorite toys and personal items, and no treats.

It was nothing like a vacation that they would have saved money for. They had long forgotten when they had their last paycheck, but my dad still remembers how his mother took several older boys on visiting day to see their dad in prison, and they brought him fresh strawberries from the market. My almost seventy-year-old dad can still smell those strawberries, and he still remembers the stern faces of the guards on that very short visit, leaving them in even greater fear about their father's fate.

Dad told me that for the whole eight days, the whole train car fed them, and a year later as they fled back, people would do it again. Their fellow travelers were themselves poor and disadvantaged people; like them they traveled to Siberia by the cheapest way possible. Each of them had their own fate and story to tell, yet most had compassionate, good hearts. That's how it always was back then! The simpler the people were, the kinder and more compassionate their hearts would be.

Then came a long layover in Novosibirsk. It was bitterly cold, the rail station was filled with people, and there was some kind of mishap with their tickets. The system was set up in such a way that it was necessary to restamp everyone's already existing tickets in order to continue. The children were loudly crying from being tired, and their mother quietly cried too. So meek and helpless, she endlessly waited in lines and humbly asked for help, moving from one window to the next. After this long ordeal, the children, frozen and hungry, were glad to be back on the train again, which they got tired of on such a long trip. Experiences pale in comparison, and now the rattling of the train was not as bad as waiting in that frigid train station under the intense loudspeaker announcing arrivals and departures nonstop.

The city of Tomsk welcomed them with Siberian biting frost and deep snow. The snowdrifts were more like snow mountains, and the cleared sidewalks resembled a maze with walls taller than everyone's head. In Tomsk, my grandmother and the children were sheltered by other Christians; the Orlov family took them in for a few days.

They also helped them to find a taxi. Their final destination was a small village of Molchanovo, deep in the Tomsk Region. It could be reached only in two ways: by a steam ferry via Ob River, but only in the summer, or by a car along the ice road when the marshes freeze over.

The children enthusiastically piled into the back seat of the Volga, and mother and baby sat in the front, next to the driver. This journey of 200 kilometers, about 124 miles, would be six or eight hours long, and the children would remember it for a lifetime. The car would veer from side to side in the deep snow, and the children became car sick and vomited to exhaustion. Once in a while the driver would stop, and the kids, pale and exhausted, would tumble out and lay their little faces right in the snow in the middle of the road. The cold would bring them back to their senses, and they would continue. They would be facing fierce winter frosts and

> They would be facing fierce winter frosts and clouds of flies and mosquitoes in the muggy summers, and they were heading toward unfinished barracks where no one was expecting their arrival.

clouds of flies and mosquitoes in the muggy summers, and they were heading toward unfinished barracks where no one was expecting their arrival.

But when the family was reunited, they felt overjoyed! Soon they were given a separate room instead of the one where three other exiled men lived together with their father. The boys started school and quickly got in touch with the locals, making friends. Several Christian women in the same village were very pleased to have the opportunity to gather for communion and to hear my grandfather teach the Word of God.

The village of Molchanovo was founded by the Russian Kazaks Molchanovsky and Lavrov in 1790. Later on an Orthodox church and a library, also known as the reading room, was built, as well as several small factories. In 1928, after Stalin's orders to begin expropriations, Molchanovsky district became part of the Gulag[6] system.

From 1927 to1929, Molchanov lumber mill was operating in the village, most if its labor force were *zeki*, prison inmates of Gulag. Later it became known as Siblag[7] (GPU/NKVD), and for-

---

[6] The Gulag was a Soviet forced-labor camp system that was used as a major instrument of political repression in the Soviet Union. It reached its peak during Joseph Stalin's reign. From 1929 to 1988 over 25 million people were part of this massive slave labor force. Millions have died from hunger, disease, and exposure.

[7] Siblag was a small cluster of forced labor camps concentrated in Siberia as part of the larger Gulag system. It had roughly 74,600 prisoners as part of its labor force.

mer Gulag prisoners known as special settlers would supply the timbers to Molchanov lumber mill.

The village of Molchanovo stood deep in the heart of endless Siberian taiga, the moist subarctic low lying forests. Everything around it was built of wood, including roads and sidewalks. Everything stood on stilts raised high above the marshlands, but you could only see it when the snow melted. From autumn to spring, the only way about the village was through the narrow passageways carved in walls of snow that were taller than your head.

The three brothers stood on the shore of the majestic Ob River, but it didn't look like a river at all. It was more like the sea or a huge lake. Half a kilometer (about a third of a mile) wide, the trees on the other side were barely visible. For the first time in their lives, they got to see an icebreaker at work. They watched in amazement as the loud and massive machine would break the thick ice into giant pieces, lumping and stacking them atop each other to reluctantly make way for the icebreaker. In springtime, the ice would float down the river, congesting on the river bend and creating a massive artificial iceberg. Airplanes would fly over and drop bombs to break it up in order to save the low-lying villages from flooding—the Ob River flooded in all directions.

As the sun rose higher, springtime woke the life-giving taiga from her winter slumber. One time the locals invited the "baptist sectarian" boys to row across the Ob in a boat to pick fresh wild garlic in taiga. By the time they decided to go back, the sky had grown dark, and one of the area's frequent summer thunder-

> Huge waves arose on the river, the boys furiously paddled with their oars, and the frightened mothers stood on the shoreline, desperately trying not to lose sight of the small boat tossed by the waves. But at least one of their mothers was praying to God for them.

storms was fast approaching. Huge waves arose on the river, the boys furiously paddled with their oars, and the frightened mothers stood on the shoreline, desperately trying not to lose sight of the small boat tossed by the waves. But at least one of their mothers was praying to God for them; God heard her prayers and saved the children in that storm. Nevertheless, there will still be many more storms ahead, which her sons and daughters must go through, and their mother will always pray for her children, day after day, year after year, patiently waiting for them, as she did back then on that high river bank.

The winters were unbearably cold, but the summers were just as unbearably hot. At least the winter was free from the flies and mosquitoes that seemed to be protecting the riches of the forests by keeping intruders at bay. Grandfather and Grandmother were living half starved. They understood perfectly well that their children were malnourished and vitamin deficient, so they would force them to go to the forest to pick berries, beautiful and abundant blueberries, lingonberries, and cranberries. Sometimes, though, it seemed that the amount of blood sucked out by mosquitoes was greater than the amount of berries eaten by the children.

With the arrival of fall, the new school year had begun. By this time, the Okara family were living in a separate apartment. One time a district commissioner came to visit them at home. A Soviet version of child welfare administration from the district, the commissioner was making sure that parents could provide decent living conditions for all their children.

Back then in Soviet times, a terrible method of putting pressure on Christians included the practice of removing the children from their homes, to keep them from being "corrupted by religion," the "opiate of the masses" (Karl Marx). Authorities would look for any reason to confiscate the children from large Christian families and then place them into countless orphanages throughout the vast expanse of the Soviet Empire. The government had a specific goal in mind: to raise all children as Komsomol[8] party members and worthy members of communist society by completely eliminating the possibility of the children to interact with each other, severing all familial ties.

My grandparents knew that had happened recently to the family of a well-known Minister Belousov from a small town in

---

[8] All-Union Leninist Young Communist League

the Rostov region. The Soviet government had confiscated all their children and placed them in different orphanages, leaving only one daughter, Natasha, with the parents.

Grandfather and Grandmother earnestly prayed for God's protection, and the answer to their prayers came just in time. It was an ordinary autumn day, the winter frost had begun, and soon the Ob River would freeze up solid until the arrival of spring. Somewhere far from the barracks where exiles lived, a number of government officials held a closed meeting.

Later that night, there was a hushed knock on my grandparents' door. An official who was unknown to them stood in the twilight. Quietly he entered the small hallway. His voice muffled, he said that there had been a meeting held by the board that night, and it had made a decision to confiscate the children of the exiled Nikolai Vladimirovich Okara due to the fact that the parents were not able to provide them with satisfactory conditions.

That was all he said. He turned and walked out, but as he was leaving, he mumbled to as if to himself, without addressing anyone specific, "The last ferry from Molchanovo to Tomsk will be leaving early in the morning." A short visit without so much as a hello and not even tea offered.

Neither of my grandparents nor the children would ever find out who this man was and why he decided to warn exiled Christians. Of course he must have been one of the committee members himself, because clearly he had participated in the meeting, but for these Christian parents, he was a messenger sent from God.

There was no time to think. Everyone understood that until the deep frost created the ice road, no one could leave the village; you could only escape by river and only now. There were only two ways to get here, ice road in the winter or the river in the summer. And the very last ferry was leaving early in the morning. There was no time for packing or long goodbyes. Grandmother grabbed whatever she could, and the children dressed in silence, whispering their tearful prayers together with their parents.

Then there was a very short farewell to their father and husband, who watched the ferry leave for Tomsk that early gray morning, feeling heartbroken and overjoyed all at the same time.

While in Tomsk, they were sheltered by the Orlov family once again. The local underground church helped Grandmother with money to buy train tickets, and they began their long journey home. Seven days, one woman with seven children. They left not knowing if they would ever see Nikolai again or how would they all survive.

But still she trusted God, believing that it must be so and that everything would work out for the best. Undoubtedly, during this slow journey, this weeklong trip, my grandmother must have searched her heart and mind in rare moments of rest as she was listening to the sound of the wheels clicking. Was this the life she had imagined for herself as she had married a young man who was an artist with a good sense of humor, who then had become a minister?

> Was this the life she had imagined for herself as she had married a young man who was an artist with a good sense of humor, who then had become a minister?

And she had become a mother, and very soon, the mother of seven children. Their daily life, as well as life in general, had been quite difficult, but it was nothing compared to the constant threats, raids, and arrests routinely practiced by the communist government. It was impossible for them to take their children to church, which took place in homes, every time in a new place, usually very early in the morning. The authorities had warned my grandfather several times, but he repeated the words of the apostle Paul: "Woe to me if I do not preach the gospel!" (1 Corinthians 9:16).

So now grandmother was left alone with all the children. However, not entirely alone, her mother, our Great-Grandmother Olya, a very strong woman, was always close by. Because of her help they survived. Great-Grandmother Olya and Great-Grandfather Fedya kept chickens and rabbits, a garden, and other farm animals. Grandma would knit wool socks and sell them. She was helping her daughter and grandchildren in any way she knew how.

My grandmother, Valentina Fedorovna Okara, is over ninety years old now. Today she lives in the US near the Canadian border, surrounded by the beauty of the Evergreen State, Washington. Her children brought her here several years ago after grandfather's death. Grandfather came back alive and well from exile, and they had more children, eleven in all—six sons and five daughters.

The persecution of Christians had ended. First their congregation had a prayer house, then in time it became possible to openly preach the gospel everywhere—a time of revival had come. The church grew and strengthened. Grandfather's sons grew up and began serving God with their father; many became pastors in other cities.

Grandmother received a medal and the honorary title of Mother Heroine, which honored mothers who gave birth to ten or more children. They were given a comfortable three-room apartment, which was the most actively visited apartment in the whole nine-story building—thank God it was on the main floor.

When the number of children, daughters-in-law, sons-in-law, and grandchildren grew to more than 100, Grandfather began to keep records and drew a large family tree. He often added branches and leaves to it with the names of new members.

Each of their children had their own journey to God, and not all of those paths were painless. The time of persecution had ended, but the attacks from the enemy on those who were called to become servants of the Living God never ceased. Grandmother and Grandfather had consecrated all their children to God, lifting each one of them with fasting and prayer. They held strong to God's promise, confessing the words, "As for me and my house we shall serve the Lord!" (Joshua 24:15 KJV). And all their children have become ministers of the Lord.

We can endlessly discuss and speculate on when and how it was possible for my grandmother to pass her living faith to her children amid such hardship.

She was uneducated and very simple, humble, kind, and often tired. It seems that her children learned everything good not through her words but by simply observing her life. Her lessons were not taught by eloquent pretense but by her own lived-out example. The children witnessed her inner strength through her unrelenting faith that was able to overcome fear and doubts. Her faith enabled her to take that very risky journey, taking her very small children along with her toward uncertainty.

She did not rely on blind chance alone; rather, she believed that her Lord Almighty, the faithful God, would always be with her.

• LIFE LESSONS •

ABOUT GOD. God the Father said this about Himself: **"A father to the fatherless, a defender of widows, is God in his holy dwelling" (Psalm 68:5).** Coming to God, we receive so much in Him. By accepting Jesus Christ we receive Him as Savior from our sins, and then we get to know Him as our brother and friend. We will never cease to discover who God is, both here on earth and through eternity.

But referring to the pages of the gospel, we find that the Son of God, Jesus, in His teachings, introduces us to God precisely as His Father. And then Jesus calls us His brothers, revealing a wonderful truth: God is our Father! Without Him we are all orphans, but through Jesus we are adopted into a family with the most kind, most loving, and most caring Father in the whole universe.

ABOUT US. Our life and our actions speak louder than words as to our identity—who we truly are. If we call ourselves God-believing people, then faith must be demonstrated by our trust in God. Faith can't hide in the heart; it must manifest itself through real choices and actions. Some believe in God's existence; they say, Yes, there is a God. But real faith is when we fully accept the truth of the Bible—the truth about God, about life, about ourselves—and we live by this faith, letting it guide us in our thoughts, decisions, and actions. **"As the body without the spirit is dead, so faith without deeds is dead" (James 2:26).**

ABOUT LIFE. One of the strongest, most incomprehensible, and indisputable things in the world is a mother's love. It is very similar to God's love—unconditional. The mother loves her little girl just as strongly as she does her drug-addicted son in prison. **"God created mankind in his own image, in the image of God he created them; male and female he created them" (Genesis 1:27).** A woman completes the perfect image of God within herself as she becomes a mother and begins to discover the unconditional and infinite love for her child.

ABOUT THE MOTHER'S PRAYER. Prayer and fasting are powerful weapons, and very often the only ones at hand. Children eventually grow up. They become independent from their parents and begin making their own decisions in life. It is heartbreakingly painful to watch them experience the real consequences of their wrong choices as they make mistakes on their way through life. But a mother's love does not give up. It continues to believe and pray for years and even decades—it is the biggest gift she can give to her children.
"Let us not grow weary in doing good, for at the proper time we will reap a harvest if we do not give up. Therefore, as we have opportunity, let us do good to all people, especially to those who belong to the family" (Galatians 6:9–10).

ABOUT FAITH. Only one kind of faith can be passed on, the living faith. Our friends can share similar beliefs with us, but all is revealed in times of testing, when everyone makes choices consistent with their deeper values. But living faith sinks deep into our souls. It pulsates in our veins. Even while being tested, it does not burn up; it becomes tempered growing ever stronger. **"That the proven genuineness of your faith—of greater worth than gold, which perishes even though refined by fire—may result in praise, glory and honor when Jesus Christ is revealed" (1 Peter 1:7).**

14

A SLOW-PACED RACE

A few years ago, my good friend started running. *Ah, at our age it is definitely too late to get into sports*, we thought as we first heard of Yulia's new hobby; my friends and I would have weekly get-togethers for a cup of tea and some desserts. But she was not at all discouraged by us not taking her seriously. She gave all of us a gift, a book about healthy eating, and continued to run. After about three years, Yulia ran her first marathon. Then she began to put together a number of charity races.

Now she had me convinced. Turns out, it is never too late to start something new. But the dream for me to run a full marathon seemed unreal. I bought myself a pair of running shoes. *Now all I have to do is start running.* But try as I may, I could not get started. Somehow I needed to get organized, to find the time, change the schedule. *What if I go to bed early and get up earlier?* I thought. But still nothing happened. In the end, I had to admit to myself that the reason this proved to be so hard was because I was already a runner in the rat race. And no one can run two marathons at once.

> I had to admit to myself that the reason this proved to be so hard was because I was already a runner in the rat race. And no one can run two marathons at once.

December came and I turned forty. *Can it be true, am I even talking about myself?*

I began to see little inconsistencies between my own reflection in the mirror and how I felt on the inside. *Oh, get over it—it's just a number. Who cares if the number is odd or even? We can count our blessings at any age.* But still, I could not sleep for those few nights. I would just lie there deep in my thoughts, listening to my girls breathing in the night and my son snoring in his room. From time to time I would cling to my husband and hug him ever so tightly, thinking, *What a good man he is* and *How deeply I love him.*

I would scroll in my head through the last years. *And today our children have grown and are already in school.* I can hardly believe how I survived those years with three little kids only a year apart as I also worked and did ministry alongside my husband.

Those heartfelt moments played inside my head like snapshots or clips from a movie, our greatest joys mixed with heartaches: Paul's asthma so terrifying, especially at night, when I would hold him up on pillows in a half-sitting position and take deep breaths as if breathing for him while he gasped for air; Katerina playing Beethoven's Moonlight Sonata on the piano for me. A sunny day when we all walk to a small neighborhood park.

Our cat named Mars, our very first pet, and despite all my protests, Arianna still kisses him. Us sitting by the ocean as I force myself to slow down this rapid pace of life. I see my children running ankle-deep in the icy waters of the ocean, and I consciously bask in the moment. Waiting for dinner guests to arrive, I ask my husband to stop by the store and buy some salad, but he comes in with a huge bouquet of red roses for me.

Life has so many parts to it, and how does it all fit into these brief moments, days, weeks?

Monday morning everyone wakes up still sleepy but I wake up with a throbbing headache. The kids are all tired, and I feel guilty (last night's guests stayed over too long, and the kids missed their usual bedtime). I help them all to get dressed, and begin to get ready for work while making breakfast. I pack their snacks and three school lunches, hurrying everyone along, and check if everyone's homework is in their backpacks. We all say a short prayer and run to the car.

We make it just in the nick of time, but we get stuck at the drop-off line, so I dropped them at the entrance instead. Three kids, three kisses each, and for the next half hour I'm in my car alone. This is my commute. I work as an accountant at a small firm in Portland. Half an hour to work followed by five and a half hours in the office, then I drive back from Oregon, where the

> Just like everyone else's calendar, every single day is scheduled to its capacity. Cleaning, washing, and cooking, as well as phone calls and endless messages— all are done in between the racing or while the kids are sleeping.

office is, back across the river into Washington, where our children go to school.

Finally we are all home, and again I hurry the children. We have only a couple of hours between school and our next event. The race continues. We eat, do homework, practice piano, read—and off we go again. Depending on the day of the week, we drive to church, gymnastics, dinner with friends, visit someone from the church, birthdays, shopping, piano lessons, and so on. Just like everyone else's calendar, every single day is scheduled to its capacity. Cleaning, washing, and cooking, as well as phone calls and endless messages— all are done in between the racing or while the kids are sleeping.

Our rare moments of pure enjoyment, when we are granted them, are like a gulp of fresh air swallowed by a deep-sea diver after a record time spent underwater. With emotions running high, eyes open wide, and through them the brain capturing and recording every little detail: blue skies, puffy white clouds, and towering evergreens on the shoreline. Another gulp. I breathe in as deeply and as much as possible to stock up on this oxygen. I fill my lungs and close my eyes—and dive back down into the depths of my familiar routine. Deep waters of everyday hustle and bustle, worries, alarms, people's problems, their pain and suffering. I want to finish everything I have started, but I want to help others even more. To do for others more, to accomplish more, listen more, hear more, see more, be more...

Oh, and yes, I want to start my running. *But not now. I'm exhausted as it is. And I don't have time.*

Wait, not having time simply isn't true. No one is deprived of time. We all are given the same amount, twenty-four hours a day. So we all need to consolidate. Usually we put on the brakes in the hospital or when everything falls apart.

I was no different. I did not press gently on my brake pedal. I had to do it passionately, like everything else I do in my life, so I wholeheartedly slammed on the brakes—stopping at full speed, I "pressed the pedal to the metal" and skidded off the road.

I had a kidney-stone blockage in my kidney a few years back. During that surgery they had found a growth in my other kidney. The Lord is merciful. The tumor was benign. Then last summer I had the stones again, but this time it did not bother me much. I was more concerned with another tumor that was accidentally found during the ultrasound. This one did not look good, so I waited anxiously for my test results.

That was the moment when everything abruptly stopped. Instead, I did a lot of soul searching. I remember that very long day in June, the day when we waited for the call from the hospital. All day long I held the phone in my hand. Later in the

> That was the moment when everything abruptly stopped. Instead, I did a lot of soul searching.

evening, my husband and I silently sat on the sofa in our backyard gazebo. The hospital finally called ten minutes before the clinic was to close, telling us that it was a simple hemangioma. We hugged each other tight and just continued to sit there.

Life is so beautiful. There are so many wonderful things in it. I have an amazing husband, beautiful children, the truly best parents, sisters, brothers, and a lot of great friends. But I feel like I am stuck in a spin cycle. I know I am definitely not meant for this, to be wrung out like socks and T-shirts. And so I simply must slow down. Reduce the speed. I urgently need to consolidate my life, prioritize stuff by order of importance, and sometimes simply say no to things.

My mind replayed the words of God. I must have heard them hundreds of times before, but now they sound alarming. "Be still and know that I am God" (Psalm 46:10). *But don't I know the Lord already? After all He is my strength, my joy, my ever-present help. Even in this spin cycle of life He is always with me.* How many times on a gloomy rainy mornings, after dropping the children off to school, I had spent the next twenty-five minutes with Him! There were times when His presence in my car was so real, so tangible, that I would tell my husband, "Today Jesus drove to work with me right here in this passenger seat."

Still, He says to me, *Stop. Be still and realize that I am the Lord of your life. Everything and everyone is under My control—relax, child, and enjoy your life.*

But, Lord, what about the marathon? How can I do all these things? How can I run without running myself over?

I know that one day I will wake up—and our children will be grown, and my husband and I will have grown old, and I hope that we won't have missed what's important.

Be still. Breathe. My grace is sufficient. Live.

Slow down your pace. Make time to notice the wonderful details of life; taste it, appreciate its beauty, listen to each child, see their art, and get to know their hearts.

Life is like a race. There is no doubt about it—life is a marathon. Apostle Paul told his apprentice Timothy that he ought to run in such a way as to get the prize (see 2 Timothy 2:1–7 and 1 Corinthians 9:24). I think I am beginning to understand that we must run our life at a slower pace, unburdened by taking on too much of someone else's load of negativity and without worry about what other people may think.

> We must run our life at a slower pace, unburdened by taking on too much of someone else's load of negativity and without worry about what other people may think.

It seems that our reward for finishing this race lies not only over the finish line but in the process itself, what I get to see and hear along the way, people who run beside me. And what I can be for them is rewarding in itself. If I want to enjoy this life, then I must run it like a marathon—slow and steady.

Now I wonder, *How long will my sneakers keep gathering dust?*

MARATHON

I am forty-two. It feels as if I have been running all my life. I don't think I know how to live any differently. To be honest, I guess I just don't want it to be any different. I feel as though I waste away in mere peacefulness and stillness. And for now I have learned how to run unburdened, enjoying my life, my journey, and the people around me.

But now for a little over a year, I have also been running in the literal sense of the word! All my adult life, I believed that sport was definitely not my thing, I would have never even dreamed of getting into an active lifestyle.

And I could have never imagined that running would bring me such joy. I never run without my headphones, and the internet is full of great podcasts, sermons, and worship—it is an endless well of wisdom! And the one with whom I love to talk is always with me too. Jogging has become my prayer closet, my secret place under the open sky—sometimes in the rain, through the park, or just around our neighborhood. But it became that a little later in the process. For the first few months when I just started, I was a painful sight. I remember the very first mile that I ran without stopping, then the first three, then five.

My first long race was 15 kilometers, and then, right before Easter, on Saturday, my little sister Irina and I signed up for our very first half-marathon.

Deciding to combine winning with purpose, or rather, adding purpose to our resolve, we wrote "Christ is Risen!" and "Jesus is alive" on our T-shirts. We ran those 13.1 miles together—and this victory was truly His.

But now, since we have started this, then we must go all the way, leaving all doubts and fears behind to run a marathon. I do not tell a soul. Only my family know about it. I think I am leaving some room for myself to back out if need be.

October 8, 2017, is the day of the Forty-Ninth Annual Portland Marathon and my very first full marathon. The air is crisp, the downtown roads blocked off, and the blasting music rocks the wee hours of the morning as this unusual crowd begins to gather. Numbers are taped to our chests with our names on them and a chip attached to our sneakers that will keep track of our progress every few miles.

My sister and I stand among thousands of other people. The energy in the crowd is overwhelming. Thousands of people with their numbers on their chests are warming up before the start, just like the two of us. We have so much in common with them, even though after today we may never see each other again. But for now, for these next four to six hours, we will all move in one direction with one goal in mind. It won't be easy for any of us, but each will have his reward at the finish line—and not just a medal but an unmatched feeling of tasting victory.

As we begin, the first hundred meters up to a few miles, I am full of energy and enthusiasm. My steps are light on my toes, my knees are high, my posture is beautiful, my face all smiles, and my hand is holding the phone counting my steps and miles. My sister and I are still joking, chatting about our children and how great it is to run together! Just ahead of us, a woman is running wearing a T-shirt with all fifty states on her back, the kind that outlines each border. Most of them are already filled in with event names and dates. We gather that she must have run a marathon in every one of those states. Being naive we think, *That is not a bad idea*, and begin to daydream about running the next marathon in some other state.

But this only lasts for the first hour, then running becomes harder, and we talk less and less.

But what took me by surprise, the most amazing thing about this new running experience, was not so much my own struggle but that I got to witness the unprecedented support from all the fans standing on the sidelines! Literally hundreds or even thousands of people took to the streets that day—they stand along our path, stretching for miles.

When our route passes through a residential area, we can see whole families sitting in their chairs, with tables and food and music blasting. A lot of them hold posters and signs with a myriad of encouraging words: "I don't know you, but I believe in you!" "Yes you can!" "Keep going!" They clap as we run past them. That is, they continuously clap, whistle, shout, and cheer us on—the whole, entire time! Nowhere and never in my thirteen years of living in America have I ever seen anything like this. Yes, Americans are very kind and polite, they always smile at you, but here their goodness is upped by more than a few levels. It feels like they personally care for all these hundreds and thousands of runners stretching over 42 kilometers!

Then comes the midstretch. We toss our hoodies to the side, lightning our load a bit. My legs begin to feel like they are made of rubber and, I want to take a short break for a minute or two. Every few miles we run through a human corridor of volunteers who hold small cups of water, electrolytes, and tubes of energy drinks so runners can replenish their lost energy on the go.

I realize how exhausted I am after about a dozen of those cups that we drank, when I have to stop for a couple of minutes, I think, *There's no way my stiff legs will be able to move again.* But I'm not alone. Irina begins to walk, then runs away—and I go after her!

The second half of the marathon is much longer and harder, miles and minutes stretch on and on, unlike the early morning part. I begin to have doubts. Picturing how I will explain this to my children, I will say that I simply didn't have enough strength to finish.

Just then, as if they can read my mind, my kids call me; all three of them begin to cheer me on over my speaker phone!

"Mom, we believe in you. You can do it. You are the sportiest and the strongest mom ever!" They keep encouraging me with words of love and inspiration, shouting over each other. A lump forms in my throat, and I want to cry from extreme fatigue and the fact that they love and support me so much is so precious to me.

So we keep on running.

Then we see an ambulance taking one of the runners who has become ill to the hospital. *Dear Lord, have mercy.*

We are nearing the end of the race, the tail end of the marathon. I feel that I no longer care whether I finish or not; I just want it to end. To be honest, I want to go home to my children and my husband. I can barely move my legs, but I can feel the raw wounds on my toes—the souls of my feet burning. My knees refuse to bend after doing it thousands of times in a row. The girl running beside us shouts, "I would rather gave birth again!" Irina and I give her a faint laugh, and we keep on running.

And still the volunteers and fans lining the road keep cheering us on continuously. They have stood there since early morning, for many long hours. And as if they could read our minds by the expression on my face, they run out onto the roadway in front of us, and looking us dead in the eyes, shout, "Come on, you can do it! You are almost there! The finish line is just around the corner!"

As I look at these people, young and old, I can no longer hold back my tears. *They have no idea who I am; why do they care if I make it or not? Have they ran a marathon themselves at some point?* I don't know any of them, but I'm so touched by every word on every poster that they hold up, every song they have played, every sincere cheer. I am so deeply touched by the fact that they have been standing on the road for so many hours, saying by their very presence, *You are on the right track—the finish line is just ahead!*

I'm at my wits' end and my strength is failing, but I see those who are ahead of me, and I simply keep putting one foot in front of the other and keep on moving.

Forward.

At times I look back to see those who are running behind me. There is no way I can quit now, because they are looking at me running and they are running after me. We all keep moving forward, awaiting our reward. We will cross that finish line to hear our names called from the loudspeakers to the jubilant cries and cheers of our families, who are waiting for us at the finish line with great love and pride.

Therefore, since we are surrounded by such a great cloud of witnesses, let us throw off everything that hinders and the sin that so easily entangles. And let us run with perseverance the race marked out for us, fixing our eyes on Jesus, the pioneer and perfecter of faith. (Hebrews 12:1–2)

This is how I see the "cloud": My life is not merely my own personal race, but it is also a race that is run in front of those who will follow behind me. And as long as we are still here, while we are still living—we all are on this journey together and capable of learning from one another. You are surrounded by a great cloud of witnesses, the people who sincerely support you, they cheer you on shouting words of encouragement from the sidelines, some from the pages of Scripture, others from across your table, your family and friends.

Just look around you. You are not alone. There is help and encouragement available—you are surrounded by this cloud! If you just begin to pay attention, you will soon discover that you too are being watched! Someone may desperately need your help and encouragement. They need for you to be their example of a life lived out through virtue by taking every day small steps of faith.

For someone, you and your life's journey make evident the truest example of faith, hope, and love.

And thus, you may be someone else's "cloud."

Olya Yarosh